WHY WE GATHER

Is Physical Gathering an Option?

Dana Carson, D.Min., C.Psy.D.Ph.D.

CONTENTS

DEDICATION

I want to first dedicate this book to my wife and friend, Rachelle Dianne Carson, my Baruch! Knitted to me in the flesh and the spirit, I could not do what I do without her.

To our wonderful children, Dana II and his wife Monet, John Anthony, Angel Naomi, Marielle Alli, and Devon Jarrod, I give my everlasting love and gratitude for their unending sacrifice of me as their father for the betterment of others.

This book is also dedicated...

> To my staff who undergirds all of my ministry endeavors.
>
> To my sons and daughter in ministry: Bishop William Kettor; Evangelist Samuel Johnson; Pastors Dr. Charles Moody, Marquet Curl, Andrew Taylor, Tyree Bearden, Clark Lazare, Diedre Williams, Mishael Carson, Sechaba Mothiane, Jeremiah Thompsons, Vitalis Nwaiwu, Kennedy Mbuya.
>
> To The R.O.C.K. church family, thank you for sharing me with the world!

INTRODUCTION

I want to tell you why I felt inspired to write this book, Why We Gather. I believe this book will serve as an apologetic discourse for the necessity of physical, in-person worship. This book is written with the expressed interest of addressing one of the most critical issues of the church in the 21st century: church gathering. While it is clear that some of the significant challenges of contemporary church society are racism, a lack of sound biblical teaching, and homosexual and lesbian involvement, church attendance seems to travel under the radar. The issues that I listed must definitely be given attention. Still, the issue of physical gathering is a low-hanging fruit that will not be addressed without a fight. After almost a year and a half of streaming their church services due to the COVID-19 pandemic, people are convinced that this can become a permanent solution to going to church. Many committed church members have become content with just streaming, giving their tithes and offerings, and either never returning to physical gatherings or occasionally gathering.

The challenge that must be addressed is the ecclesiastical purpose of the church and the biblical definition of the ekklesia. The church fulfills the role of spiritual Israel as a kingdom of priests (Exodus 19:6). However, Israel was not Israel unless they were in the corporate gathering. Israel could not be defined by individuals but by the whole. In this book, I will examine the concept of gathering and the significance of the church corporately gathering as it relates to being called "the people of God."

Many of us are who we are today not necessarily because we caught what was being taught in our churches, but simply being a part of the church community made the difference. When I was a child, I remember going to church up to the 4th grade until we moved into a new, predominantly white neighborhood that eventually led to white flight (all the whites moved out when we moved in). It wasn't until the 7th and 8th grades that I met my friends, Larry, Floyd, and Robert Jr. Skinner, who had a family gospel quartet group called "the Jordan Travelers." They were like the Jackson 5; their entire family could sing. As a 13-year-old and having a People's Peter temperament (you'll have to read my book Let's Get Real to get a full explanation of what that means) or a sanguine personality, I was enamored by my friend, Larry, and his family. I gravitated to Larry, who was my age, and then to his family. Larry lived across the street from our school, Earle Elementary School, on the southside of Chicago in the Englewood district. Sometimes they would sing at neighborhood talent shows and events. My friend Larry sang like Michael Jackson, so if you know me, you know I was blown away by this church family, whose father also happened to be the pastor.

My life was changed forever after I began going to the Greater Pleasant Valley Missionary Baptist Church with them. The pastor, Robert Skinner, Sr., a very quiet man, was also very warm, caring, and welcoming; he treated me just like the family. This experience, having up-close access to the man of God, changed me as a 13-year-old. I would always see him, and I mean always, reading the Bible. Initially, he was a bi-vocational pastor, but eventually, he just pastored as the church grew. I attended church with them every Sunday until I was 16 and had my driver's license. My dad would allow me to drive his car on some Sundays to church. My father had a Cadillac, so what an incentive to go to church; I was driving in style!

Eventually, I got my mother and father back in church. They stopped attending church after we moved from 45th and Oakenwald to 62nd and Wood St. In our former church, my father was a deacon, even though he was not a man of spiritual discipline. My mother was in the choir, even though she wasn't really a singer. But it was the church that helped our family gather in a special space together on Sundays. The Skinners tried to help me get into their singing group inspite of my inability to hold a note. I wanted to sing so bad, because it was so awesome to be able to sing during the time of Motown. I was so motivated, I taught myself to sing, and Floyd Skinner would give me some tips from time to time. Floyd recommended me to another church family group, the Woolfalk Singers. I auditioned, and it didn't go so well, because I couldn't keep my key. As expected, they were disinterested, despite how bad I wanted to be in the group. But because I knew Joey Woolfalk, who was a sometime lead singer but primarily the guitar player and background singer, the group allowed me to play congas after I talked my dad into purchasing me some. After that, Joey and I became great friends.

Now I went through all of that to tell you how important the local church gatherings were in my life. Mind you, I had no interest in the Bible and only listened to the preaching when it was whooping time at the end of the message. I never read the Bible. In fact, I never owned one, but I was a part of the physical church gathering. That church gathering provided me with the foundation in the church that I have now. While I was not a serious Christian, I grew up in the church, which caused me to have a favorable opinion about the church. I believe that it was the plan of God for me to have met the Skinners, the Woolfalks, and others who provided me with an awareness of the church, which prepared me for the call of God that eventually brought me to where I am today.

I can't imagine where I would be if I didn't have access to the physical gathering of the church. I never would've known that as a young person, totally disinterested in church, God was doing clandestine work in my life beyond my own awareness. This is similar to how He handled the Apostle Paul, who was being prepared for what God had called him to while persecuting Christians. As soon as Paul received his Damascus Road experience, He was sent to Ananias and the church (Acts 9:10-22).

In my 36 years of pastoring, I have seen that most of the people who become members of the church and establish a strong membership in the local church had some contact with a local church as children. God states that when His law is forsaken, it will have an impact upon the third and fourth generation of children (Exodus 34:7). When we compromise physical gathering, we are also compromising our children's spiritual future. Our decision to turn away from the church and spiritual things hands them totally over to the culture of the internet and unmonitored online activities and information. Physical gathering is necessary if we desire to give birth to the next generation of Kingdom-minded followers of Jesus Christ. Hence, it is also important that Christian parents insist that their children attend church with them. Without this mandate, your children will not participate in church. They will have a total disinterest in the local church due to all the other interests they have. Therefore, you must train up a child in the way they should go, and when they are old, they will not depart from it (Proverbs 22:6).

Once again, I believe this book will serve as an apologetic discourse for the necessity of physical and in-person worship. This book will help pastors and church leaders prepare a sound argument for physical gathering. I believe that the content written within the pages of this book will be in demand for the next century of Christianity if there is a 'next' century. I believe that we are the generation that will usher in the return of Christ and the subsequent eschatological events. This book will help you understand, once and for all, the purpose of the church and why God commands that we physically gather.

Why We Gather

THE SIGNIFICANCE OF COMMUNITY

The value of family and community is immeasurable. Many of us are who and what we are or had an opportunity to be based upon our family and community interactions. Sociologists and behavioral experts state that each of us, in terms of who we are as individuals, exists based upon the cause and effects of family and community interaction. While our identity is associated with the interaction and upbringing of a healthy and functional home, which provides us with the five fundamental impartations of the parental and child relationship (security, belonging, acceptance, identity, and affirmation), it also involves external interaction of community.

You and I are the offspring of our parents and grandparents with whom we share DNA. Thus, our personality and proclivities of behavior are based upon our nature or, better said, temperament, which is our blood flow. While DNA deposits are the foundation of who we are and play a role in who we become as people, another huge component provides the bedrock of who we are and become, and it is called "nurture." We are, as people, a combination of nature (DNA) and nurture (community). Nurture is better understood as environmentalism or the traits gathered and developed through the mentorship and interaction between the person and the community.

Community can be simply defined as "those who played a significant part in our overall development, such as parents and family, extended family, teachers, coaches, mentors, etc." Community is the sponsors who helped shape us by providing mentorship, direction, and critical interactions. However, community is not simply composed of people – it includes environment such as economics, class, race, and ethnicity, just to mention a few. All of these dynamics play a huge role in our development. I bet as you read this book, you can reflect on the people in your history who have made an enormous impact on your worldview, good or bad. You can remember the conditions in which you were brought up and reared. Why do I bring this up? Because I want to stress just how important the interaction with our parents, family, and community is and its role in our development.

Family is vital because of the necessary touches and impartations that are made in the family. Maslow categorizes "belonging" as the third-tier need of the human being in his hierarchy of needs, following physiological and safety needs. All three of the first five of Maslow's hierarchy of needs deal with interaction with others. The interaction with our family taught us the values and principles that help to guide our lives. The values and principles that guide our lives were not disseminated to us through technology but through interaction. Family was developed through interaction – warm hugs, smiles, and the unique and priceless moments you experienced with your family members. All of us have those times that are stored in our personal family data based on moments in family history. When we recall them, at weddings, family reunions, funerals, birthday parties, etc., the recollections tend to go like this: "Do you remember when we were...?" These moments in time and history were based upon interaction, touch, and impartation. But some of us also remember the touches in family trips where we visited relatives in other cities, states, and sometimes countries. Why did we make those trips? After all, we talked on the phone, and long-distance was the next best thing to being there. We made those trips because, to perpetuate family, our patriarchs and matriarchs ensured that we had physical interaction with family members. These visits helped us develop a sense of family and community.

I don't know about you, but for me, the relationships that I have with family are only those with which I had interactions with either in childhood or adulthood. I'm close to my family that I have kept in touch with over the years. I don't have a sense of community with those I have not kept in touch with because we had no interaction. For example, my cousin, Dale Thompson who lives in Memphis, Tennessee, and is close to my age, is my father's sister's child whom we visited annually from Chicago. Thus, today, we have a tight relationship because of interaction that brought about a deeper sense of family and community. As a result, I am there for her in ways that I can't be for other family members, including her siblings, because beyond name similarity, there is not a connection.

The nuclear and the extended family are significant relationships that are developed by interactions. A nuclear family is a place where we learn to build the concept of community, especially among siblings. What is a nuclear family? The traditional nuclear family is a family that consists of a father, a mother, and their children. As a formal definition of family, it stands in contrast with the single-parent home and the extended family or a family with more than two parents. However, a nuclear family or the two-parent home and their children can also include a primary residence that consists of stepparents and stepchildren. There are, however, ethnic differences. Europeans have established the traditional nuclear family model, but many other groups such as the Native Indians, Latinos, Africans, and others operate from the extended family model, which includes extended interaction in the person's development. Grandparents, uncles, aunts, cousins, and even surrogate relatives are seen as a part of the primary family community.

My upbringing included a hybrid between the nuclear and the extended family model. My older brothers, Willie Lee Carson and John Carson, Jr., who were both tremendous athletes, taught me how to play sports, particularly baseball. My brother Willie taught me how to pitch and I had the opportunity to play baseball with them as kids. Though they were older than me and out of the house by the time I was born (I was the un-expected child, the one not planned for, but came by the will of God), we were close because of interaction and gatherings. I had the esteemed privilege of offici-ating both of their funerals. My big sister was kind of a tomboy; she would fight for me and my cousin Willie James Jones, who died at 14, but who also fought for me when I was a little kid because we were family and stuck together. We were taught as children that fam-ily is primary in your life – you help family, share with family, and don't fight family. We were taught not to fight each other. Still, if anyone messed with anyone that resided at our place of gathering, they were es-sentially messing with everyone that represented our family and community.

When I grew up on the southside of Chicago, we lived in two places – 4529 S. Oakenwald St. and 6231 S. Wood St. I still remember our phone number (312) 776-3775. I remember these things because not only was family important, but the place or geography where family took place was equally important. My parents were very intentional about building a sense of family and the importance of having a home. But they also taught us to protect, clean, and take care of where our family lived and that our home was our safe place. Thus, no matter what happened, home represented safety and protection. I know in our contemporary world, we've placed significance on friends, family, and community through social media. Unfortunately, while I find tremendous value in social media platforms, they can never be a meeting place for authentic community and family. Authentic family and community only happen in physical spaces in repetitive cycles. A sense of family or community can occur in long-term hospitalization, senior citizens living, and even prison because of the physical interaction. My point is that family and community happen in a place or geography.

2 SOCIAL DISTANCING AND CHURCH

I just discussed how important social impartation and physical interaction are, but as you know, we are coming through one of the deadliest pandemics in world history. Unlike some pandemics that plague a country or continent, COVID-19 has impacted the entire globe. Because of the COVID-19 virus, millions of people have lost their lives due to this deadly virus. At the beginning of the contagion, the world was in chaos and panic because it seemingly came out of nowhere. And, of course, in harmony with human nature, everyone looked for someone to blame. This is reminiscent of the Genesis narrative and the contamination of humanity by the most explosive and consequential virus that ever hit creation, death. Because of this pandemic, every man was born in sin, and when asked by God what happened, the inquiry resulted in blame. Adam blamed Eve, and when God asked her, she blamed the serpent. So it was with the pandemic, blaming China, laboratories, ill-advised experiments, and so on, and so on.

COVID-19 was killing millions of people worldwide. The first and most intelligent way of handling this very contagious virus that we knew very little about, was to engage in social distancing pandemic protocols. Social distancing in public health is also referred to as "physical distancing." It is a set of non-pharmaceutical interventions or measures intended to prevent the spread of a contagious disease by maintaining physical distance between people and reducing the number of times people come into close contact with each other.[1] Social distancing was a very responsible decision to make to try and preserve and protect human life.

Social distancing was recommended by the Center for Disease Control (CDC) and executed on the state and local levels. This governmental agency was tasked with the assignment of working with top-level doctors in infectious disease control. In a collaboration between CDC, disease control experts from around the nation, the U.S. Department of Health and Human Services (HHS), and the Department of Homeland Security (DHS), they had to determine essential or non-essential businesses based upon human survival. The Department of Homeland Security developed a list of essential critical infrastructure workers to help state and local officials as they worked to protect their communities while ensuring continuity of functions critical to public health and safety and economic and national security.[2] They determined that workers in the following settings are most commonly deemed "essential" across the states: grocery stores, pharmacies, medical supply stores, convenience stores, pet stores, hard-

1 Wikipedia.com, *Social Distancing*, Retrieved from https://en.wikipedia.org/wiki/Social_distancing.
2 Department of Homeland Security. *Advisory Memorandum on Identification of Essential Critical Infrastructure Workers During COVID-19 Response*, Retrieved from https://www.cisa.gov/sites/default/files/publications/Version_3.1_CISA_Guidance_on_Essential_Critical_Infrastructure_Workers_0.pdf

ware stores, office supply stores, and liquor stores. Essential (critical infrastructure) workers include health care personnel and employees in other essential workplaces (e.g., first responders, utilities). Frontline essential workers are firefighters, police officers, corrections officers, food and agricultural workers, United States Postal Service workers, manufacturing workers, grocery store workers, public transit workers, and those who work in the educational sector – teachers, support staff, and daycare workers. State and local officials made the final determinations for their jurisdictions about critical infrastructure workers.

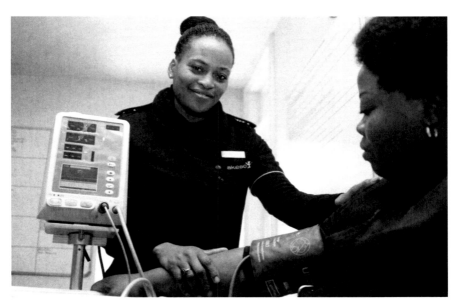

Health care workers, emergency responders, and essential workers helping keeping us safe.

The governmental agencies, I believe, did an incredible job of trying to manage this extemporaneous crisis. However, the initial declaration of what was important and essential did not take the church into consideration. Thus, the church was listed as a non-essential business. While this makes good scientific sense, considering the spread of this contagious disease, the CDC had to go back and reclassify the church and allow the churches to gather with their worship production teams to stay in contact with their parishioners. This determination of the church being non-essential struck a mighty blow to the significance of the church.

I believe that this was no accident because we must remember that Satan is the god of this world system (2 Corinthians 4:4). The world's systems are under the sway of Satan, and he controls its worldview and determinations. But God, who is rich in mercy and kindness, ensured a connection between church shepherds and their flock or membership. Thus, the church took to the airways of digital technology, which caused an economic blast of increased revenue for an already bustling industry. Facebook, Instagram, YouTube, and digital technology companies, such as internet providers, were catapulted to overnight revenue bliss. They developed strategies never to lose their market share as the industry continued to offer technology like StreamYard, Restream, Zoom, and the like. The church, during social distancing, had to figure out how to deliver worship services and all other ancillary services online through technology such as Zoom.

To cut to the chase, the church had to reorganize and become a digital church, requiring that the church have the video equipment, technology resources, and a congregation that would make the digital adjustment. Because many churches were not prepared for this transition and were convinced that the shutdown would only last for 4-6 weeks as initially stated by national and local governmental officials, many churches folded and had to declare bankruptcy. Other churches were attempting to adjust and had a huge learning curve but were determined to survive. They maintained enough people and resources to keep things going. But then, other churches were already transitioning to incorporate technology into their services. These churches were tasked with the challenge of upgrading their technology and being creative in their ministry offerings.

Filming worship for livestream at Bethel Church in Austin, TX.

I believe that the church being classified as non-essential had a lasting psychological and spiritual effect on society. This pandemic, which I refer to as a plague, brought about one of the most challenging times in modern Christendom. The church had to undergo and is still sorting through a mental transformation regarding what was considered normal operations. The church is in a state of waiting and wondering as it will take years to recapture the ecclesiastical influence it once had, pre-COVID, if, in fact, it gains that level of influence ever again. Many of our church leaders have gone through psychological challenges as we have had to rearrange our lives and adjust how we execute our callings. Thus, worship, in the context of social distancing, brought about new challenges for the church in membership accountability and financial sustainability.

3

GATHERING AND THE OLDER TESTAMENT

When we discuss physical gathering and its importance, I think about the Garden of Eden and the third heaven. The Garden of Eden was a gathering place upon the earth. God created it in time, matter, and space; the scriptures declare that in the beginning, God created the heavens and the earth (Genesis 1:1). This statement declares that existence came into being through the simultaneous appearance of time, matter, and space after God spoke. What's interesting, as it relates to physical gathering, is the fact that everything existed in the mind of God before it manifested in reality. The scriptures declare that Christ was slain before the foundation of the world (1 Peter 1:20, Revelation 13:8). This suggests that before Christ was a physical reality, He was a non-physical reality in the eternal mind of God. However, the design of God could not be fully executed in the spirit realm; there had to be a physical manifestation.

The sphere in which the plan of God takes place is a physically manifested sphere; thus, He created the heavens and the earth. The heavens consist of multiple spheres. The Hebrew word for "heavens" is שָׁמַיִם, pronounced shamayim (shah-ma-eem), which means "heavens or sky." In biblical Hebrew, -im denotes plurality; thus, shamayim is more than one heaven. Though God created multiple heavens, He only created one earth. Thus, in Hebrew, the earth is הָאָרֶץ, which is pronounced ha erets (ha eh'-rets); the definite article suggests a single earth. Therefore, God created the heavens and the earth as physical realities in time, space, and matter.

Each of the heavens became a gathering place for the creation of the universe. The first heaven is the sky we behold from the earth. The psalmist wrote, "the heavens declare Your handiwork..." (Psalm 19:1). The second heaven is the abode of evil principalities and powers, spiritual wickedness in heavenly places. Thus, it is the gathering place of fallen angels (Ephesians 6:12, Revelation 12:7; 14:6). The third heaven is the abode of the angels of God, where God established His visible throne among created beings (2 Corinthians 12:1, Isaiah 6:1-3).

In the books of Isaiah and Job, we also notice that in the abode of God, the angels were physically gathered around the throne of God (Isaiah 14:12-15, Job 1-2). Physical gathering is a place of accountability; thus, the angels, even Satan, must report physically to an omniscient God! It is a place where service is determined and assigned, and it is a place of reverence and worship. It is also a place of humility, as depicted in the six-winged seraphim.

Now you may be asking what is the point? The point is that in the Older Testament, God established creation in physical gatherings. Adam, Eve, and the animals gathered on earth in the Garden of Eden, and the angels gathered in the heavens. But everyone had a gathering place. In fact, it was not just a gathering place, it was a gathering among compatible beings. Adam tried to gather with the animals, but they were not compatible with him. Thus, God said, "It is not good for man to be alone" (Genesis 2:18). The framework of the design of creation is for gathering and community. We were created to gather!

In the book of Genesis, we discover the significance and the design for created beings to gather not simply among human beings but even in the animal kingdom. The animals were created to gather. It is dangerous in the animal kingdom or in the wild for certain animals to be separated from their community. When animals are separated from the community, they become easy to capture and be eaten by other animals. Gathering is crucial for some animals that they hunt communally; together, they trap their next prey.

When we examine the book of Genesis, we discover that gathering was the lay of the land. The first family gathered, so when Cain killed a family member (his brother), it was such a violation of community and gathering that he was punished and marked as a consequence (Genesis 4:15). Community is essential, and, early on, we see that it can be challenging to establish harmony in community. But Cain's punishment was banishment from his community (Genesis 4:12).

When we continue to explore the Bible through Genesis and beyond, we know that the sin of Adam passed to all of humanity, creation was disrupted, and evil entered the world. All of the imaginations of humans were wicked and evil (Genesis 6:5). Yet humanity grew and grew and created communities of gatherings on the earth. Eventually, God flooded out the earth, and all perished except Noah and his family (Genesis 7:1-24). What saved Noah and his family? Physical gathering – they gathered in an assigned place by God – the ark. The ark was the assigned place of God, and it included fellowship with his family, eight in all. Eight in biblical numerology is the number of "new beginnings." Thus, God used these eight gathered people, who came into the ark, to continue human existence. I think we all can agree that physical gathering is significant, because only those who heard the voice of Noah entered the ark and were saved.

We discover during the antediluvian period that humanity began establishing community through physical gathering and choosing chiefs, rulers, or those who were in charge, such as Nimrod and the Tower of Babel (Genesis 10:1-11:32). Together, humanity attempted to build a resistance to God's judgment. They unified and built the Tower of Babel.

Physical gathering is a critical piece in the scriptures. When God established covenants with people in the Older Testament, the places were always marked by

God and the person as significant. We can understand the beginning of God's covenantal gatherings by examining the life of Abraham, the progenitor of Israel. God told Abraham to leave his place and community for God to establish in him a new community and a new place (Genesis 12:1-3). Thus, Abraham built a community of offspring, starting with Isaac, then Jacob (Israel), and then the children of Israel, who continued to develop and fulfill the promise that God made to Abraham concerning his offspring and the Promised Land.

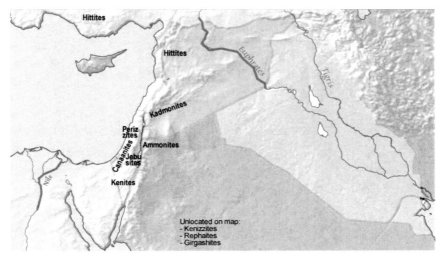

Map showing one interpretation of the borders of the Promised Land, based on God's promise to Abraham (Genesis 15).

Israel and Physical Gathering

Physical gathering as an act of worship and religion in the Older Testament began with Israel as a covenant people of God. God delivered Israel, His people, from Egyptian bondage and brought them out with a mighty hand (Exodus 6:6). He opened the Red Sea to destroy their pursuers and created Israel as a people for Himself. Israel was the only people of God, who had been redeemed through 10 plagues, the blood of a lamb, and the crossing of the Red Sea. Israel became a nation, born through Passover, and was referred to as God's firstborn (Exodus 4:22). As God's people, Israel was known for its gatherings, including feasts, sabbaths, worship, witness of the law, war, and weddings. Israel was not Israel in isolation, nor could it be defined by an individual. Israel was identified as a whole, as one people – the people of God with a corporate identity. They were referred to as the assembly, not the church assembly, but the congregation in the wilderness (Exodus 16:2, Acts 7:38).

In the Older Testament, two different words are used to denote gatherings of the chosen people or their representatives: (1) edah, meaning "congregation," and (2) qahal, meaning "assembly." In the Older Testament, the Hebrew word for assembly is qahal. The Septuagint, the Greek translation of the Hebrew Bible, translated the word qahal into ekklesia. Ekklesia means "church or Messianic Community." Sunagógé is the usual translation of edah. Both qahal and ekklesia, by their derivation, indicate calling or summoning to a place of meeting, but there is no foundation for the widespread notion that ekklesia means a people or a number of individual men called out of the world or mankind. Qahal or ekklesia is the more sacred term denoting the people in relation to Jehovah, especially in public worship. The qahal was an assembly that gathered around the Older Testament covenant, which bound them to Torah. Qahal is the assembly or gathering of the people of God. Thus, Israel was considered the assembly only when they gathered collectively. Israel could not be defined by the individual, only by the corporate.

When Israel as an assembly gathered for different purposes, they could only be defined by their God-given structure and systems of worship that governed them as a body. What the individual did impacted the body, not simply the individual. As a result, personal and private sins had corporate impact. Thus, both corporate and private sins were dealt with at one central place, the Tabernacle. Israel's existence revolved around the Tabernacle, the physical meeting place of God, over which He appointed apostolic leadership, such as Moses, Aaron, and the Levitical priesthood. God referred to Israel as מַמְלֶכֶת כֹּהֲנִים (mam-la-kah ko-hen-eem) or a kingdom of priests. Thus, everyone in Israel was considered priests, with the Aaronic priesthood existing as the highest order of protocol, followed by the Levitical priesthood, which served in the Tabernacle and eventually the Temple. In our terms, the Israelites were the lay priests. As a nation, they were considered mediators of the Kingdom of God upon the earth.

So Israel could not be defined as an individual, only as a gathered community. Yet, the individual was defined by the corporate, not the corporate by the individual. For example, when Miriam created havoc and desired a meeting with God around Moses, she had to come to the door of the Tabernacle. Immediately, she was struck with leprosy and had to be excommunicated from the corporate so that she did not infect the community (Numbers 12:1-10). Israel, with its vast, multimillion population, was defined by community, not individualism. Achan was another person who impacted the community's success by his individual action, because the whole was affected by the individual (Joshua 7:10-26). The entire community of Israel was impacted by the actions of one man, and the consequences of one man affected his whole family.

Israel was a community comprised of individuals, not individuals who were a community in and of themselves. Israel initially was not an ethnic group; they were just a Semitic tribe. In fact, God stated that before He cut covenant with them as a people, they became a kingdom of priests, a community that represented God (Exodus 19:6). Israel was and is a covenant people who are the prized possession of God the King. They were God's authorized dealers or representatives of the Kingdom of God. No man could come into the Kingdom of God unless they were engrafted into the community through the adherence of the Torah, circumcision, feasts' observance, and participation in tribal worship. Even in disobedience to God, Israel was dealt with corporately; the punishment was corporate exile. Likewise, Israel's restoration would be corporate. Israel was a community of physical gathering to such an extent that God gave them their own disbursement of land. Israel was connected to a geography, Canaan. God's people cannot be God's people disbursed around the world without physically gathering in a sacred place. The physical gathering made them the assembly, a congregation in the wilderness, and a kingdom of priests.

A 1692 map of Canaan

The Rise of Judaism and Gathering

Protocols in place governed the call and election of Israel as God's chosen people. Israel met at the Tabernacle, the Temple, and eventually, in the Newer Testament, the synagogue. However, Israel wasn't Israel when they could not gather physically, which was the case in exile. In exile, the terminology changed to "the Jews." The word "Jew" is used to describe those who practice Judaism or those whose ancestry includes Judaism. "Judaism is an Abrahamic ethnic religion comprising the collective religious, cultural, and legal tradition and civilization of the Jewish people. Judaism is considered by religious Jews to be the expression of the covenant that God established with the children of Israel. It encompasses a wide body of texts, practices, theological positions, and forms of organization. The Torah is part of the larger text known as the Tanakh or the Hebrew Bible, and supplemental oral tradition is represented by later texts such as the Midrash and the Talmud. With between 14.5 and 17.4 million adherents worldwide, Judaism is the tenth-largest religion in the world."[1]

From a more specific and formal perspective, Judaism began with Ezra and his writings as he encouraged Israel, after they returned from Babylonian captivity, to put away their strange wives and return to the book of the Law, the Torah, or the instructions of God. His campaign suggested that Israel had begun to backslide after she compromised Torah and tried to be like the heathen polytheistic nations around her. He argued that the fall of the northern kingdom in 722 BC at the hands of the Assyrians, the fall of the southern kingdom at the hands of the Babylonians in 586

---

1 Google Arts & Culture. *Judaism*, Retrieved from https://artsandculture.google.com/entity/judaism/m03_gx?hl=en

BC, and the Persian exile beginning in 539 BC were the result of Israel compromising their relationship to Yahweh and Torah. During Ezra's quest to push Israel back to the Torah and the Mishnah, the Babylonian Talmud emerged and became the central teachings of the rabbis. The Talmud was written to ensure that the Torah would not be violated anymore, causing Israel into exile again. Thus, they put laws on top of the Torah. Over time, Torah got lost, and the Mishnah and Talmud were front and center in Judaism.

So, after the Babylonian exile, they sought to rebuild their meeting place, the Temple, which was destroyed during the exilic period of Israel but restored during the time of Haggai and Nehemiah. Israel discovered that they were not Israel in terms of being the mediators of God's Kingdom on earth. Without a Temple, they could not fulfill their end of the covenant and obey Torah. They struggled to try and be the people of God in exile because of the challenge of freedom of worship and obedience to the Torah.

As God's people, the protocols of the Kingdom that governed them centered around gatherings. They gathered to hear the Torah, as declared by Moses and the high priests, in physical gatherings, not private sessions. They physically gathered three times a year (Deuteronomy 16:16) in convocations or feasts: Passover, Weeks or Pentecost, and Tabernacles. They gathered regularly to hear the words of the Torah to ensure that they did not stray from the parameters of the covenant. Israel was a gathering people due to the covenant of God; they were the assembly of God. Yet, the gathering of Israel was only official when the proper protocols were in place, such as the senior leader and/or the high priests or the Levitical priesthood. The gatherings had to be surrounding Torah, the instructions of God, also known as the right way to live a life pleasing to God. The calling and election of Israel were always about carrying the presence and purpose of God among the nations. Henceforth, they were a holy people who were considered the possession of God (Exodus 19:1-6).

Israel was required by God to participate in convocations. In Hebrew, the word "convocation" is miqra (mikraw). In Hebrew, this word means "rehearsal." The term miqra also means to "read and understand" the laws of Elohim. The word "holy" in Hebrew, in this context, means qadosh. In Hebrew, this word means to be set-apart or to be holy/sanctify for God. The word "convocation" means firstly to practice, secondly to read and understand the laws of Elohim. In a nutshell, the term "convocation" means to set apart an appointed time (Sabbath/festivals) to God and to read and understand His laws so that you can use His laws in your life (practice them). These convocations were so significant that God repeatedly communicated His expectation for Israel to participate in these gatherings (Exodus 12:16, Leviticus 23:1-3, 7-8, 20-24, 27, 34-36, Numbers 28:16-31; 29:1, 7).

The physical gathering of Israel was for the purpose of establishing corporate identity and community. In the wilderness, the children of Israel physically gathered as an act of protocol. Chosen leadership was present and provided instruction based upon Torah. Direction by Yahweh was given through His servant Moses and a cloud by day and a pillar of fire by night. When they physically gathered, there was a time of confession and sacrifice through the Levitical priesthood. The only ones that God spoke to as individuals were senior leaders such as Moses. The called leader was the mouthpiece of God to the assembly, because God did not speak to the individuals but to His chosen leadership. They, in turn, spoke to the people on behalf of God. Thus, when Israel physically gathered, they did so under chosen leadership.

Physical gathering was necessitous for Israel to be the people of God – it dictated their movement and position before God. The tribes were situated for physical gathering. They traveled with the Tabernacle based upon allotted spaces based upon the geographical location assigned by God. Physical gatherings were essential to the building of community within Israel. Even in the divided kingdoms after Saul, David, and Solomon, under the leadership of Rehoboam and Jeroboam (southern and the northern kingdom), there were still clan gatherings. Israel had to remain in formation and physically gather either as the northern kingdom or the southern kingdom.

As an act of worship, physical gatherings were the design of God for all His created beings. It is the place of worship and community building, and it is the place of both vertical and horizontal relationships. Fallen humanity, Israel, and the angels were all created with the need and design to physically gather. God is a God of unity through community. He is one God in three Persons; He is the Triune God. God is a God of community who has created humans to be born at least on the surface in community. But His spiritual people are a people who worship in the unity of community.

Why We Gather

4 GATHERING IN THE INTERTESTAMENTAL PERIOD

The Intertestamental Period was a significant time in world history, especially to Israel and Judaism. What is the Intertestamental Period? The Intertestamental Period is the 400 years that transpired between the book of Malachi and the ministry of John the baptizing one. These 400 years are also known as "the silent years" due to a belief that God was silent during this time. With no official scriptures or evidence of prophets speaking, this period is often overlooked. Though God may have seemed silent, He was anything but inactive.

There were no canonical writings produced during this period. Yet, there were significant historical writings written that serve as a bridge between the testaments. This group of books is called The Apocrypha and some historical accounts of God's people, including 1 & 2 Maccabees. Although this material presented an accurate portrayal of history, this work is not regarded as scripture because theologians determined there was no prophetic inspiration. Instead, God was exceptionally moving, preparing His people for the coming of His Son, the Messiah.

During that era, Aristotle developed his laws of thought and logic that are still with us today. His most famous student, Alexander the Great, laid the groundwork for the Newer Testament to be written as he attempted to hellenize the entire world. Alexander the Great and the Hellenization of the world had a tremendous impact upon Judaism. Hellenization forced the Jews to translate the Hebrew scriptures into Greek, known as the Septuagint. The Greeks greatly influenced God's people with language and culture—which is why our Newer Testament was written in the Greek language—and remained an influence well after other nations took over.[1]

Alexander on a mosaic from Pompeii, an alleged imitation of a Philoxenus of Eretria or Apelles' painting, 4th century BC.

1 Orlando, First. *What is the Intertestamental Period?*, Retrieved from https://www.firstorlando.com/stories/what-is-the-intertestamental-period/

At the beginning of this period, Judah was under the rule of Persia, who allowed God's people to return to the land of Judah and resume their form of worship. This ended their time of exile and made way for the restoration and the rebuilding of the Temple. In 331 BC, Persia was conquered by Greece under the reign of Alexander the Great, who ruled Judea until 164 BC. After this chapter of Greek rule, other rulers reigned over the Jewish people and persecuted them. Around 63 BC, Rome conquered the land, removing any independence from Judea. Rome brought law to the people of Judea, offering governmental stability that promoted peace yet little freedom. The Roman rule also brought roads to the entirety of the empire, connecting the land in the way of such vital importance as God prepared His people to fulfill the mission of spreading the gospel throughout the nations.[2]

Over these 400 years, we see God's chosen nation cultivating a new identity. The Hebrew people walked through a season in which they were tested and challenged by foreign cultures and ruling authorities. Yet, through this season, God preserved and prepared His people for the coming of King Jesus.[3] The Intertestamental Period also taught us once again the necessity of physical gathering to create community. During this time, from Temple reform and rebuilding, the Jewish people started a new form of physical gathering.

The ravishing of the Temple forced the Jewish people, God's chosen people, the seed of Abraham, to create a new form of corporate gathering known as "the synagogue." The term "synagogue" has a Greek origin (synagein, "to bring together") and means "a place of assembly." Synagogues are consecrated spaces used for the purpose of prayer, the reading of the Tanakh

2 Ibid.
3 Ibid.

(the entire Hebrew Bible, including the Torah), study, and assembly. However, a synagogue is not necessary for Jewish worship. Halakha (Jewish law and jurisprudence based on the Talmud) holds that communal Jewish worship can be carried out wherever ten Jews (a minyan) assemble.[4] The concept of synagogue revolves around the idea of physical gathering, and there must be 10 Jewish men at least 30 years of age to teach in the synagogue. The Jewish people understood that they could not be the people of God dispersed around the world; there had to be a sense of physical gathering; Israel was not Israel unless she gathered.

Jewish Religious Groups of the Intertestamental Period

Just as in the time of the Tabernacle and the Aaronic priesthood, Israel had to gather. There had to be official leadership present in the gathering and the gathering had to reflect Torah. During the Intertestamental Period, a new form of leadership emerged in the absence of formal leadership resulting from the multiple exiles of Israel and after the disassembly of the Aaronic priesthood. The new form of leadership that developed was the Pharisees and the Sadducees. A more resistant group also emerged, the Zealots, of whom Judas Iscariot was a member. While many other sects developed during these intertestamental transitions, the Pharisees and Sadducees were the dominant sects. The Pharisees were critical to physical gatherings because of the nature of the leadership void they represented.

Who were the Pharisees? The Pharisees were rabbis who believed the Temple was unnecessary and Torah was the most essential aspect of Jewish life. They worshipped in synagogues, interpreted the Torah, and

4 Wikipedia. *Synagogue*, Retrieved from https://en.wikipedia.org/wiki/Synagogue.

most notably, believed in the importance of oral law (Torah she'bal peh). This group thought that God gave the Jews instructions orally at Mt. Sinai and those laws were just as important as the laws written in the Torah. The Pharisees were lower-class citizens and lived in the worst conditions in Jerusalem. The Pharisees didn't really like living under Roman rule. The Pharisees' Judaism is what Jews practice today. They cannot make sacrifices at the Temple and instead worship in synagogues.[5]

Who were the Sadducees? The Sadducees were the wealthy upper-class Jews, who were involved with the priesthood. They completely rejected oral law, and unlike the Pharisees, their lives revolved around the Temple. The Sadducees' job was to make sacrifices and maintain the Temple's purity. Although the Sadducees were the most involved with the Temple, they were also the most Hellenized Jews and respected Greco-Roman civilization and rule. The Pharisees and Sadducees made up the Sanhedrin, a council of seventy men who made all of the decisions for the Jews. The tie-breaker was the high priest, who was called the nasee. In modern Hebrew, nasee means "president."[6]

A Sadducee, illustrated in the 15th-century

5 URJ Heller High. *The Pharisees, Sadducees, Essenes, and the Zealots*, Retrieved from https://hellerhigh.org/2017/03/10/pharisees-saddu-cees-essenes-zealots/
6 Ibid.

While the Pharisees and Sadducees are clearly presented in the Newer Testament, another sect gathered in the great scramble for Jewish identity in a Roman-ruled world was the Essenes. Who were the Essenes? The third sect, the Essenes, actually left Jerusalem to live in a kibbutz-like compound in Qumran (near the Dead Sea). Their secluded desert community was dedicated to prayer and study in preparation for the return of the Messiah. They were obsessed with purifying themselves for the Messiah and constantly went in the mikvah, the Jewish ritual bath. The Dead Sea Scrolls, used by the Essenes, have been discovered and used in some of the newer Bible translations (e.g., Holman Christian Standard Bible). The Dead Sea Scrolls were found in Qumran and are the oldest copies of the Tanakh ever discovered. Who were the Zealots? The Sikarim were zealots who completely opposed Roman rule. The Sikarim was ready to kill all the Romans and any Jews who didn't help them overthrow the Romans. The word "sikarim" actually means "little dagger;" this group was named for the daggers they would use to kill people.[7]

Qumran cave 4, where ninety percent of the scrolls were found

7 Ibid.

The Jews' Strategy to Survive

When we look at the formation of these groups, we discover the methodology utilized to cope with the Jewish scramble for religious and ethnic identity. The strategy of Jewish survival during the diaspora of the Jewish period included the necessity of physical gathering. The four sects gathered around their belief in transitional survival based upon their interpretation of the Torah. All of the groups were based upon apostolic leadership structure and hierarchy. While we discover these groups in the Newer Testament, they were given birth during the intertestamental struggle for identity and cultural presence. Regardless of the challenge, Israel understood the great necessity of physical gathering, even if she had to do so in a smaller context than Temple worship. God's people were not God's people until they gathered.

When we consider apocalyptic literature, the hope of Israel is the hope of national identity and gathering as a united people. The Prophet Ezekiel, in his famous prophetic utterance known as the "valley of dry" bones, spoke of the necessity of the restoration and reunification of Israel as a people as an end-time sign (Ezekiel 37:1-14). The punishment and consequence for Israel for not being the people of God and having their physical gathering distorted by the compromise of the leaven of the heathen world was the Jewish diaspora of the Older Testament. However, God promised Israel that they would have a prophetic day of gathering. Around this promise, the concept of "the Day of the Lord" was formed. God promised that the throne of David would be restored, and the Messiah would sit upon it. God would rule through His people, Israel, and the Gentile nations would have to bow to His majesty. The hope of Israel was physical gathering (Acts 1:6).

The number one weapon of Satan is to divide and conquer, because he knows the plan of God is physical gathering (Mark 3:24). Thus, Satan looks for opportunities to isolate the people of God so that he may devour the people of God. He attempts to draw the sheep from the herd so that they become totally vulnerable to destruction. Physically gathering provided instructions, protection, accountability, empowerment, and unity through community. The people of God understood that their greatest strength was the physical gathering so that they may hear the Word of the Lord through those who God had ordained to speak and teach on His behalf. Thus, we discover that what kept the Jewish people from totally collapsing during their transitions and Jewish scramble was their ability to physically gather. Physical gathering was in Nehemiah's mind as he restored the walls of Jerusalem. Physical gathering was in the mind of both Haggai and Zechariah as they wrote about the significance of the house of God.

God's people cannot sustain their religious presence and integrity without physical gathering. Whenever God's people were not allowed to gather, they always developed a strategy to gather. To create a hermeneutic of isolation or physical distance as a means of corporate worship is to develop a hermeneutic of Satan, a doctrine of demons. God's people have always been called to a physical gathering to hear the united voice of God in the assigned place of God through the representative of God. We must never forget the value and preeminence of physical gathering as a strategy of long-term sustainability. Physical gatherings are a strength mechanism that promotes the power and unity of community, which cannot be established in social distancing.

The prophetic promise of God to the Prophet Ezekiel was to bring Israel back to their homeland as a people, which is the concept of corporate gathering. Of course, in 1948, Israel became its own independent nation. Subsequently, the Jewish people from the diaspora began to return to Israel for corporate and religious identity. And God has protected them as a mighty nation in the physical gathering.

Why We Gather

5 GATHERING AND THE NEWER TESTAMENT

The foundation of the Newer Testament is the Older Testament and the Intertestamental Period. As we have seen in a consistent thread of thought among God's original people and the Word of God, physical gathering is the way of the Kingdom of God. The Newer Testament gospels communicate the ministry of Jesus, His message, His ministry, His methodology, and His movement, which was the Kingdom of God. However, in the gospel of Matthew, he began with a roll call of Jesus' lineage, which is related to physical gathering and identity.

Jesus the Messiah was descended through 42 generations to become the incarnate Son of God among men. The concept of redemption begins with community – Mary and Joseph and their family lineage. Jesus was a Jew according to His upbringing and context – not an American nor a European (John 1:11). According to Jewish prophecy, Jesus was born a Jew, raised within Jewish culture, died within the Jewish context, and resurrected. The 21st century has brought us to a place where we must begin to appreciate the cultural context of Jesus and abandon the anti-Semitic thoughts and beliefs of Romanization through Westernization. When Jesus was lifted out of His Jewish culture, He was then interpreted through the lens of European culture, which affirmed the supposed cultural superiority of the Gentiles. We have not fully understood His ministry context because of our ignorance of *Yeshua Hammachiach* – Jesus, the Jewish Messiah of the world.

I want to point out several significant aspects of the Jewish context and culture of Jesus the Messiah that help us understand His approach to religious duty and service as the representative of God.

1. **Jesus was born, raised, and died a Jew.** The birth narrative in Matthew connects Him to 42 generations. Later, the wise men declare that He was born King of the Jews (Matthew 2). Jesus was born within the Jewish context from the parameters of the Ten Commandments and Mishnah concerning betrothal and kiddushin, which signifies sanctification, separation, and the setting aside of a particular woman for a specific man. According to Mishnah, adultery during betrothal is a more severe sin than adultery after marriage. Mishnah prescribes four types of death for the guilty person: stoning, burning, beheading, and strangling. A man who has had sex with a betrothed woman was subject to the same penalty as one who has sex with his mother – stoning. Someone who has sex with another man's wife is subject to strangling. Thus, the Bible clearly states that Jesus the Messiah was conceived by the *Ruach Ha Kadesh*. The virgin birth is based upon divine prophecy in the Jewish context. The

Prophet Isaiah said in chapter 7:14 that a "virgin" (almah: a young woman of marital age; can also mean a young unmarried woman of good reputation, virgin) shall conceive a son. The Newer Testament uses the word parthenos to describe Mary. Unequivocally, this word means "virgin; one who has not known a man."

The Prophet Isaiah prophesies about the Jewish Messiah – His name would be called "Immanuel" or God with us – "us" being a term that also implies physical gathering. Joseph's behavior showed that he accepted Yeshua as his son. According to the Mishnah, if one said, "This is my son, he is to be believed." He then has the right of inheritance. Thus, Jesus was the acknowledged and legal son of Joseph. This fact entitled him to the throne of King David, for Joseph was a descendant of David. Matthew traced 42 generations of Jewish history to establish the right of inheritance to Jesus. The prophecy of a king speaks of the day of physical gathering for the Jewish people; they were to experience, once again, unity through community.

Jesus was circumcised on the eighth day according to Jewish Law in Torah (Luke 2:21). He was also named within the framework of Jewish culture, which was the right of the father. A name was thought to convey character, identity, and destiny. During this time, the four most popular boy names were Yeshua (Jesus), Simon, John, and Joseph. In Jewish culture, the father would name the child based upon the perceived character and purpose of the child. Note that Leah named her first four sons – Reuben, Simeon, Levi, and Judah, demonstrating Jacob's disdain for her, though he still engaged in sexual intercourse with her. The angel told Joseph that the Child should be named Yeshua, which means "Yahweh saves or salvation."

Jesus, at age 5, like the other Jewish boys, learned and memorized the Hebrew scriptures and later the oral traditions (Mishnah). At age 12, Jesus became a son of the commandments, referred to as a bar mitzvah in our modern-day society. Thus, the Bible records that Jesus demonstrated His knowledge of the Hebrew scriptures (Torah) when He was in the Temple, astonishing the Pharisees and other Jewish leaders with His understanding of the law (Luke 2:46-48). He learned His earthly father's trade and worked with him — His father (Joseph) was a carpenter.

The Bible is very strategic in providing us with information about Jesus' childhood. First is the information surrounding His birth. Then, the Bible gives us a snapshot of Him at about two years old or younger, again demonstrating His Jewish context. The wise men gave gifts of gold (symbolizing kingship), frankincense (symbolizing priest, *pontifex*, bridge-builder; he that makes way for men to access God), and myrrh (symbolizing one who is to die) (Matthew 2:11-16). Next, we are told about Jesus being left in Jerusalem but found three days later in the Temple teaching (Luke 2:41-50).

The next time we see Jesus is at the age of 30. He was subjecting Himself to whom some called a prophet, John the baptizer, with the spirit of Elijah. John must be understood within the context of Jewish culture as the forerunner of Christ and the breaker who contains the sheep until the coming of the King (Micah 2:13, Malachi 3:1; 4:5-6). Why did Jesus appear at the age of 30? Was there any significance? Of course! According to Jewish custom and culture, a man did not qualify to speak in the synagogue or present a lesson on the law until He reached 30. When the voice from heaven could be heard at His baptism, and the dove appeared, those were divine confirmations of Christ or Yeshua Hammachiach, known from Psalm 2:7. Every Jew embraced this psalm as a description of the Messiah. This prophetic understanding of the Messiah can also be seen in Isaiah 42:1 (suffering servant, I'm well pleased), culminating with Isaiah 53. Jesus speaking in the synagogue at age 30 was His first Kingdom ministry action, and His reading of Isaiah 61 confirmed His Jewish Messiahship.

2. **Jesus, the cross, and resurrection must be understood in light of the Tabernacle and the feasts.** The Tabernacle and the feasts were at the heart of Jewish worship, covenant, and practice. Of course, both the Tabernacle and the feasts were characterized by physical gath-

A model of the Tabernacle showing the holy place, and behind it the Holy of Holies

ering. One cannot understand the model of worship presented in the scriptures without knowledge of the Tabernacle and the feasts. The Tabernacle provides us with a picture of redemption, and the feasts provide us with the practice of redemption. The three courts in the Tabernacle are a portrait of the ministry of Christ. First is the brazen altar, where people confessed their sins daily and offered sacrifices based upon the nature of the sin. The brazen altar was in the outer court; also in the outer courts was the laver, the bowl where the Levitical priesthood would wash their hands and see their reflection before serving the people at the brazen altar. The second area of the Jewish Tabernacle was the inner court or the Holy Place. The inner court housed three furnishings: the altar of incense, the candelabra, and the table of showbread, all speaking to the prophetic ministry of Jesus. The next court was the Holy of Holies or the Most Holy Place, where the Ark of the Covenant was housed. The priests entered the Most Holy Place once a year. A veil separated the priests from the ark that God Himself opened during Yom Kippur or the Day of Atonement. Yom Kippur was practiced in conjunction with the feasts. While the brazen altar represented the conviction and confession of personal sins, Yom Kippur represented Israel's national or universal sins. When an aerial view is taken of the Tabernacle courts, we see the image of the cross.

The journey of Passover was connected to the Holy of Holies, the Passover Lamb, and the scapegoat. Jesus was tried from court to court, searched and examined but to no avail. Pontius Pilate washed his hands of the matter and declared he found no fault (John 19:4). Thus, Christ was now qualified, according to Jewish Law, to be the Passover Lamb that would take away the sins of the world. Passover is comprised of three feasts: (1) the Feast of Passover teaches us that the Lamb had to be sacrificed for the sins of the world; (2) the Feast of Unleavened Bread teaches us the Lamb must not have any blemishes (leaven), and (3) the Feast of Firstfruits teaches us that the Lamb is to be the first of them that slept but then resurrected from the dead. When Christ died on the cross, the veil was torn in the Temple, demonstrating that man can have access to God by way of the resurrection of Christ (Matthew 27:51). Jesus' death provided access to the King and His Kingdom. Thus, the same power that raised Christ from the dead quickens our mortal bodies and gives us life (Romans 8:11)!

God in Himself represents the unity of community. In the incarnation, He represents the unity of community with mankind through physical gathering. God came down and became what man was but never stopped being who He was; humanity was added to His divinity. Within the

DNA of Jesus, we discover the significance of physical gathering. He was born as a Jew, lived as a Jew, died as a Jew, and was raised from the dead as a Jewish Savior of the world.

Jesus' cultural context totally saturated the ministry, the methodology, the mission of Jesus, the Jewish Messiah. The ministry, the Personhood, and the nature of Jesus surround physical gathering, for the Word became flesh and dwelt among them (John 1:14). For Jesus, the Tabernacle and the feasts represented places that the people of God gather. The ministry of Jesus was about the physical gathering of God. While God had somewhat of a distant relationship with humanity, God decided or designed redemption not to be done at a distance but through physical gathering; thus, God became man. Physical gathering was a consistent methodology of God for the salvation of His people.

3. **Jesus' ministry was built upon physical gathering; He was God in the flesh, and He established the unity of community through the 12 disciples.** The physical gathering of the 12 provided the Jesus movement, the Kingdom of God in the Now, with a foundation. I believe that no one would argue with the fact that the only way the disciples could become who they became was through physical gathering. Because of the physical gathering of the 12, they are heralded as figures who had an enigmatic experience that cannot be duplicated because of their physical gatherings with Jesus. Jesus clearly presents us with the model of discipleship; He spent three years preparing the 12 for their Kingdom mission. We don't find one day where the disciples

were not gathered with Jesus for an impartation. There are some things you just can't get at a distance; Jesus mentored these men according to the rabbinic traditions, which required physical gathering.

The ministry of Jesus mandated physical gathering for discipleship; His style of ministry culminated with the gathering for the last supper and the upper room gathering for Pentecost. Both events could not take place without physical gathering. The Last Supper/Passover Meal was meant to take place as a community or in physical gathering. The Jewish Seder Meal is a unity of community experience that takes place in a gathered context. The Last Supper was not designed for individuals but for the community of faith. We are called to be a remembering community through participation in the corporate Lord's Supper.

The second gathering event that marked the birth of the church was the Feast of Pentecost, which was one of the most attended feasts among the Jewish people. Thus, the Holy Spirit fell in the gathering; they were all in one place on one accord (Acts 2:1-4). The unity of community was the prerequisite of Pentecost. The theme of the Pentecost narrative is based upon physical gathering, not due to the technology of the day but according to the design of God. Just as human beings cannot be birthed through normal processes except through physical gathering, so it is in the birthing of spiritual things. There must be a coming together or physical gathering. As a result of the gathering at Pentecost, the church is given birth. The church is the prophetic announcement of Jesus according to the gospel of Matthew. Jesus stated that He would build His church in the future (Matthew 16:18-19). Ekklesia, therefore, suggests the new people of God, the new Israel.

4. **The church is the gathering community of God, just as Israel was the gathering community of God.** The church was established on the Day of Pentecost as the repository of the saved (Acts 2:47), which states the Lord added to the church daily. Just as there is no Israel without gathering, there is no church without gathering. When we don't understand the role of Israel, we can't understand the role of the church, because the church has taken the temporary position of Israel during this dispensation.

The gospel of Matthew records that while Jesus and the disciples were overlooking the gods of this world, Jesus asked the disciples a question,

"Who do men say that I, the Son of Man, am? (Matthew 16:13)." Thus, after the flattering positive connection to John, Elisha, and Jeremiah instead of the lord of the flies, Beelzebub, Jesus asked the billion-dollar question, "Who do you say that I Am?" Thus, Peter received the revelation (ἀποκαλύπτω), which means "to remove a veil or covering to make known what was unknown before," and said, "You are the Christ, the Son of the Living God." Then Jesus stated to Simon Peter, son of Jonas, "You are now Peter," which means identity was now associated with the revelation of Jesus. The name "Peter" in Greek is Πέτρος, which means "little stone, a stone, never a rock (Homer); it is a large stone, a piece of fragment of a Rock that a man may throw." Then Jesus stated, "But upon this rock (πέτρα: a projecting rock, cliff, boulder, or massive rock), I will build (οἰκοδομέω: construct) My church (ἐκκλησία). The ekklesía means "to be called out." It was used for the congregation of the called people who assembled for a free state's public affairs. The body of citizens called together by a herald (kerux) or proclaimer, preacher, crier, constituted the ekklesia. The term "church" is a term of physical gathering, which means the church is not the church unless it is in gathering. You cannot define the church in individualistic terms; it is a community or a group term.

Defining the Church

When it comes to the necessity of physical gathering, I believe that it is necessary to take a deeper dive into the nature and purpose of the church from a biblical perspective vs. how people define their own personal need to gather or not gather. Many people believe that physical church attendance is unnecessary due to access to streaming technology, which becomes a theology from below vs. a theology from above. In the model prayer, Jesus stated that we should pray "let your will be done on earth as it is in heaven" (Matthew 6:9-10), which suggests a theology from above, not one from below. Let's further examine the concept of church to determine whether it was designed to be a place of physical and spiritual gathering or can the church be the church on the internet alone.

The term "church" is the translation of the Greek word *ekklesia* (εκκλησία). The term speaks of an assembly duly summoned; the essence of the word is a physical gathering of a specific group of people selected by God. The εκκλησία is a group or assembly of persons called together for a particular purpose. The term appears only twice in the gospels (Matthew 16:18; 18:17) but frequently appears in the book of Acts.[1] The term is also mentioned in the Pauline epistles and most of the remaining Newer Testament writings, especially the Revelation of John. John speaks of the dispensa-

---

1 Biblia. *A Church*, retrieved from https://biblia.com/factbook/A-Church

tion of the seven churches of Asia Minor, which sums up the entire church age or the age of the Gentiles. The term "church" is rooted in both the biblical Hebrew language and the *Koiné* Greek language. I previously mentioned its Hebrew counterpart, *qahal*, which means "a special assembly," or "to assemble together in a great body, either upon a civil or religious account." It is an assembly that gathered for worship, war, weddings, and witness of the law.

Ekklesia (εκκλησία) is a Greek compound word, which is from *ek*, which means "out" and *kaleó*, which means "to call," so *ekklesia* means "to call out." This word in the singular appears approximately 80 times, and in the plural, 35 times in scripture.

Theologian and religious author, Thomas Oden (*Life in the Spirit*), posits that the apostles used the word *ekklesia* to refer to the act of a gathering or assembly of persons brought together by the Lord's own calling to hear the gospel and sit at the table with the Living God. The *ekklesia* was also used in political ways. It spoke of a chief governor choosing his special cabinet of delegates and empowering them for service. Thus, those who are a part of the *ekklesia* have been granted the power of attorney to act on behalf of their King and Kingdom. Therefore, the church is the official representative (i.e., embassy) of the Kingdom of God upon the earth.

I thought it would be helpful to include the following article that discusses the historical usage of the term as it relates to its companion term of the Older Testament:

> "In the NT, the word is applied to the congregation of the people of Israel (Acts 7:38). On the

other hand, of the two terms used in the Older Testament, *sun-a-gógé* seems to have been used to designate the people from Israel in distinction from all other nations (Acts 13:43, Matthew 4:23; 6:2, James 2:2, Revelation 2:9; 3:9). In Hebrews 10:25, however, when the gathering of Christians is referred to, it is called not *sunagógé*, but *episunagógé*, with the preposition, *epí*, meaning "on or upon," thus it's translated as "the assembling… together." The Christian community was designated for the first time as the ekklesia to differentiate it from the Jewish community, *sunagógé*, in Acts 2:47.

The term *ekklesia* denotes the Newer Testament community of the redeemed in its twofold aspect. First, it refers to all who were called by and to Christ in the fellowship of His salvation or the church worldwide of all times, and only secondarily to an individual church (Matthew 16:18, Acts 2:44, 47; 9:31, 1 Corinthians 6:4; 12:28; 14:4-5, 12, Philippians 3:6, Colossians 1:18, 24). It is designated as the church of God (1 Corinthians 10:32; 11:22; 15:9, Galatians 1:13, 2 Timothy 3:5, 15); as the Body of Christ (Ephesians 1:22, Colossians 1:18); as the church in Jesus Christ (Ephesians 3:21); and exclusively as the entire church (Ephesians 1:22; 3:10, 21; 5:23-25, 27, 29, 32, Hebrews 12:23). Secondly, the Newer Testament churches, however, are also confined to particular places (Romans 16:5, 1 Corinthians 1:2; 16:19, 2 Corinthians 1:1, Colossians 4:15, 1 Thessalonians 2:14, Philemon 1:2); to individual local churches (Acts 8:1; 11:22, Romans 16:1, 1 Thessalonians 1:1, 2 Thessalonians 1:1). *Ekklesia* does not occur in the gospels of Mark, Luke, John, nor the epistles of 2 Timothy, Titus, 1 and 2 John, or Jude. The term *ekklesia* speaks of persons legally called out or summoned (Acts 19:39, of the people); and hence also of a tumultuous assembly not necessarily legal (Acts 19:32, 41). In the Jewish sense, it represents a congregation, assembly of the people for worship, e.g., in a synagogue (Matthew 18:17) or generally (Acts 7:38, Hebrews 2:12 quoted from Psalm 22:22, Sept.: Deuteronomy 18:16, 2 Chronicles 1:3, 5).[2]

This article assists us in understanding that when Christ spoke of the church, He spoke of a new people of God who would represent Him in the world – a people who He was now calling to a sacred and governmental assembly of worship.

The Church: The Assembly of God

The use of the word ἐκκλησία in the Newer Testament is somewhat dependent upon the Older Testament and the Greek world. In the former, the Hebrew word עֵדָה (edah /ay·daw/) designated the congregation or the assembly of the Israelites, especially when they were gathered for religious purposes and specifically

2 Thomas C. Oden, *Life in the Spirit: 3* (Systematic Theology), (Harper, 1992).

to hear the law (Deuteronomy 4:10; 9:10; 18:16; 31:30, Judges 20:2, Acts 7:38). In the Greek world, the word "church" designated an assembly of people, a meeting, such as a regularly summoned political body, or simply a gathering of people.[3] The word is used in a secular way in Acts 19:32, 39, 41. The specific Christian usages of this concept vary considerably in the Newer Testament:

1. In analogy to the Older Testament, it sometimes refers to a church meeting, as when Paul says to the Christians in Corinth: "... when you assemble as a [in] church" (1 Corinthians 11:18). This means that Christians are the people of God, especially when they are gathered for worship.

2. In texts such as Matthew 18:17, Acts 5:11, 1 Corinthians 4:17, and Philippians 4:15, "church" refers to the entire group of Christians living in one place. Often the local character of a Christian congregation is emphasized, as in the phrases, "the church in Jerusalem" (Acts 8:1), "in Corinth" (1 Corinthians 1:2), "in Thessalonica" (1 Thessalonica 1:1).

3. In other texts, house assemblies of Christians are called churches, such as those who met in the house of Priscilla and Aquila (Romans 16:3, 1 Corinthians 16:19).

4. Throughout the NT, "the church" designates the universal church, to which all believers belong (Acts 9:31, 1 Corinthians 6:4, Ephesians 1:22, Colossians 1:18). Jesus' first word about the founding of the Christian movement in Matthew 16:18 has this larger meaning: "I will build My church, and the powers of death shall not prevail against it."

---

3 Faithlife Sermons. *What Is A Church?* - https://sermons.faithlife.com/sermons/584647-what-is-a-church

The church, both as a universal reality and in its local, concrete expression, is more explicitly designated in Paul's writings as "the church of God" (e.g., 1 Corinthians 1:2; 10:32) or "the church of Christ" (Romans 16:16). In this way, a common, secular Greek term receives its distinctive Christian meaning and sets the Christian assembly/gathering/community apart from all other secular or religious groups. The church is a living organism in the spirit realm that gathers in the physical realm. To understand and define the church outside of the necessity of physical gathering is not to discuss the church of the Living God at all. It is clear from the Newer Testament, as a whole, that the Christian community understood itself as the community called into being by God's end-time act of revelation and divine presence in Jesus of Nazareth. So Paul tells the Christians in Corinth that they are those "upon whom the end of the ages has come" (1 Corinthians 10:11). That is, God had visited His creation, called out a new people from both Judaism and the Gentile world, empowered by His Spirit, to be present in the world, sharing the good news (gospel) of His radical, unconditional love for the world (Ephesians 2:11-22) and the arrival of His Kingdom.

The gospels tell us that Jesus chose 12 disciples who became the foundation of this new people. The correspondence to the 12 tribes of Israel is clear and shows that the church was understood both as grounded in Judaism and as the fulfillment of God's intention in calling Israel to become "a light to the nations, that my salvation may reach to the end of the earth" (Isaiah 49:6, Romans 11:1-5). It is this recognition that allows Paul to call this new Gentile-Jewish community, this new creation, "the Israel of God" (Galatians 6:15-16). In this new community, the traditional barriers of race, social standing, and sex—barriers that divided people from one another and categorized them into inferior and superior classes—are seen to be shattered: "There is neither Jew nor Greek, slave nor free, male nor female; for you are all one in Christ Jesus" (Galatians 3:28, NIV). The church is a community that is born in the Spirit and established through the cross.

This broad understanding of the church is further amplified throughout the Newer Testament through various concepts and images, each revealing a particular facet within the early church's understanding of itself, its nature and mission. The church saw itself as an institution of gathering, even to the point that they risked their lives to gather and hear the teachings of Jesus through His apostolic messengers.

The Church as the Community of the Spirit

The scriptures present the church not as a secular gathering but a spiritual gathering rooted in the power of the Spirit that gave rise to a new creation or community of the Spirit. Luke, known as the gospel of the Holy Spirit, presents the church as that community of people in which and through which the Spirit of God is working. The church is seen as an extension of Jesus of Nazareth. In this gospel, John the baptizer announced the coming of one who would baptize with the Holy Spirit (Luke 3:16). In Acts, this promise is seen fulfilled in the outpouring of the Spirit (1:5; 2).

Depiction of the Christian Holy Spirit as a dove

As Jesus was empowered for His mission by the Spirit (Luke 3:21-22), the early Christian community was empowered for its witness in the world (Acts 1:8). Like Jesus, the Man of the Spirit, is confronted at the outset of His ministry with significant obstacles (the temptation, etc. – Luke 4:1-13, 28-30). Likewise, the church, as the community of the Spirit, faces the temptation to yield to pressures that would compromise its mission (Acts 2:12-13; 4:1-22; 5:27-42). As Jesus, empowered by the Spirit, proclaimed the good news and touched the lives of people with reconciliation, release, and restoration (Luke 4:18-19), so the church is empowered by the Spirit to become a community of caring and sharing (Acts 2:43-47; 4:31-37). Like Jesus, the Man of the Spirit, reaches out to the weak, poor, and rejects of the Palestinian society (this is a special emphasis throughout Luke's gospel), so the community of the Spirit is concerned with concrete human need (Acts 4:34-35; 6:1-6).[4] These parallels could be multiplied; they illustrate Luke's understanding of the oneness of Jesus' ministry with that of the church. The latter is the extension of the former; yet, it is impossible without the foundation provided in Jesus' own ministry.

As the assembly of the Spirit, the church speaks of the church's unique call and mission to represent Christ upon the earth, even against opposition and forces of evil that will attempt to stop the church from executing its mission. When we look at the church's mission, it makes more sense why the church must physically gather. The church's mission is a corporate mission that involves worldwide communities of local churches attempting to proclaim the message of the Kingdom of God, as Jesus preached it to the world, and then shall the end come (Matthew 24:14). If we define the church by what we get out of it, then it stands

---

4 Larry Murray. *Church – Following Jesus.* Retrieved from https://following-jesus.blog/2020/03/19/church/

to reason why people would not see the significance of physical gathering and sink their teeth into the streaming network for a smorgasbord meal. However, the church is not simply about who offers the best family services and convenient times.

We gather to be equipped for the work of ministry (Ephesians 4:11-12); we engage in perpetual ministry that increases with age and does not decrease (1 Corinthians 15:58). Unfortunately, the church has become a sociological institution built upon politics, economics, and religious ideologies vs. the assignment of opening the gates of the Kingdom of God and ushering people into a relationship with Jesus, the Jewish Messiah of the world. The call of the church is evangelism and discipleship, and individuals are equipped for that work through the ministry of the local church and through worship and discipleship that empowers personal witness. When the church is not the place of equipping and empowerment, it is easy to interpret that there is no need to physically gather. Not only does the church provide equipping for the work of ministry, but it also provides corporate identity through the unity of community. When we gather, we are encouraged to be who we are in the world, not compromise ourselves to fit in the world.

The Church as the Body of Christ
The biblical concept of the Body of Christ is a Pauline analogy that speaks both of physical gathering and community. Paul, among the Newer Testament writers, is the only one who spoke of the church as "the Body of Christ" (1 Corinthians 12:27, Romans 12:5, Ephesians 1:22-23; 4:12, 1 Corinthians 10:16-17; 12:12-13) or as "the body" of which Christ is the "head" (Ephesians 4:15, Colossians 1:18). The origin of this way of speaking about the church is not clear. Among sev-

eral suggestions, two are particularly revealing about Paul's thought:

1. **The Damascus Road experience.** According to the account in Acts (9:3-7; 22:6-11; 26:12-18), Jesus identified Himself with His persecuted disciples. By persecuting these early Christians, Paul was actually fighting against Christ Himself. It is possible that latter reflection on this experience led Paul to the conviction that the living Christ was so identified with His community that it could be spoken of as "His body," that is, the concrete expression of His real presence.

The Conversion of St. Paul , 1530-1535

2. **The Hebrew concept of corporate solidarity.** Paul was a Hebrew of the Hebrews (Philippians 3:5), and his thinking was thoroughly Jewish. In that context, the individual is largely thought of as intimately tied into the nation as a whole; the individual does not have real existence apart from the whole people. At the same time, the entire people can be seen as represented by one individual. Thus, "Israel" is both the name of one individual and the name of a whole people. The "servant" of Isaiah 42–53 can be both an individual (Isaiah 42; 53) and the nation of Israel (Isaiah 49:1-6). This idea of corporate solidarity (or per-

sonality) is the background for the intimate connection Paul makes between "the first Adam" and sinful humanity as well as between "the last Adam" (Christ) and renewed humanity (1 Corinthians 15:45-49, Romans 5:12-21).

The reality of the intimate relationship between Christ and His church is thus expressed by Paul as the organic unity and integration of the physical body (Romans 12:4-8, 1 Corinthians 12:12-27). For Paul, the Lord's Supper is a specific manifestation of this reality: "The bread which we break, is it not participation in the body of Christ? Because there is one bread, we who are many are one body, for we all partake of the one bread" (1 Corinthians 10:16b-17).[5] Since this is the case, Paul argues that all the functions of the body have their legitimate and rightful place. Division within the body (i.e., the church) reveals that there is something unhealthy within. This image of the church as the "Body of Christ" lies behind Paul's repeated call for and insistence upon unity within the Christian community.

The equation of Christ and the church in this image of "body" leads to a very particular understanding of the nature of Christian existence. Paul speaks of the life of faith as life "in Christ." To be "in Christ" is to be a "new creation" (2 Corinthians 5:17). But for Paul, this is not just an individual experience, a kind of mystical union between the believer and Christ. For in a real sense, to be "in Christ" is at the same time to be in the church. To be "baptized into Christ" (Galatians 3:27) is to become one with a community where the traditional barriers of human society are overcome—"for you are all one in Christ Jesus" (Galatians 3:28). Again, to be "in Christ" is to be "baptized into one body" (1 Corinthians 12:12-13),

---

5 Shawn Strout. *"Jesus' Table Fellowship, Baptism, and the Eucharist."* Anglican Theological Review, vol. 98, no. 3, Anglican Theological Review, Inc., July 2016, p. 479.

for "you are the body of Christ and individually members of it" (1 Corinthians 12:27). There is then, for Paul, no such thing as a Christian in isolation, nurturing an individual relationship with Christ. To be a Christian is to be incorporated in a community of persons who are growing toward expressing, in their "body life," the reality of Christ, fleshing out this reality in everyday life and work.

It's clear that the Body of Christ speaks of the unity of community as the church. We must strive to gather physically, or we will lose our corporate identity, become like the world around us, and have no power to transform anyone, because we ourselves will be one with the world. When we come out from among them, we come to each other unto Christ (2 Corinthians 6:11-18).

The Church as the Temple of the Living God
Paul refers to the church as the Temple of God. "In his attempt to overcome the divisions within the church at Corinth, Paul pictured the church not only as the Body of Christ, but also as God's Temple, as the dwelling place of God's Spirit (1 Corinthians 3:16-17). Contrary to much interpretation, this passage is not concerned with individual Christians as "temples" of God but with the Christian community, in its common life and work, as God's Temple. For Paul, the church at Corinth, and the Christian community everywhere, is God's option, God's alternative to the brokenness and fragmentation of human society. Therefore, to be involved in destroying that Temple—by disunity, lack of concern and love, etc.—is to invalidate the potential of the church as God's option and to bring upon oneself the judgment of God (1 Corinthians 3:17). The community of believers is "God's building" (1 Corinthians 3:9), and Christians are responsible for being involved in its

construction with "materials" that endure (1 Corinthians 3:10–13).[6] Indeed, Christians themselves are seen as the building blocks which form the structure of "a holy temple in the Lord" (Ephesians 2:20-22).

The roots of the idea that a community of people can be the dwelling place of God's presence go back into the pages of the Older Testament and are mediated to Paul through Jesus' own understanding and that of the earliest Christian community. In the faith of ancient Israel, the Tabernacle/Temple was considered the visible sign of God's presence among His people (Exodus 25:8; 29:42-46, Leviticus 26:11-12, Ezekiel 37:27). That is why there was such despair among the exiles in Babylon. The Temple had been destroyed. How could the people still come into the presence of God? Yet, side by side with this exclusive location of the presence of God in the Temple, there was the frequent recognition that God's presence with His people could not be localized (Isaiah 66:1-2). The law would no longer be engraved on stone, signifying God's presence upon the ark of the covenant in the inner sanctuary of the Temple; instead, God says, "I will write it upon their hearts;

---

6 Murray, *Church – Following Jesus.*

and I will be their God, and they shall be my people" (Jeremiah 31:33).

Jesus pushed this concept further. In His discussion with the Samaritan woman, He rejected the idea that proper worship of God is tied to a particular sanctuary and affirms that God is present wherever people respond to Him in authenticity and integrity (John 4:20-24). Jesus also envisioned the final dissolution of the Temple in Jerusalem (Matthew 24:1-2, Mark 13:2, Luke 21:5-6). Stephen, in his defense before the Sanhedrin (the Jewish council), took a similarly critical attitude toward the Temple (Acts 7:48, "The Most High does not dwell in houses made with hands") and cited Isaiah 66:1-2 for support. John interpreted Jesus' word about the destruction and subsequent raising of the Temple (John 2:19) as referring to Jesus' own body and His resurrection. Since the church came into being as a result of the resurrection, the identification of Jesus' resurrection body as "temple" and its correspondence to the new community established through that event lay close at hand. Whether Paul was directly dependent upon these ideas is difficult to determine. What is clear is that he was part of a tradition that increasingly understood God to be present among His creatures in and through a living community of people, consecrated for a particular purpose, like the Temple of old.[7]

The Church as the People of God

The phrase "the people of God" is both an Older Testament and Newer Testament description. It was a common strand of Israel's faith that she became the people of God because He chose her to be His own possession (Exodus 6:6-7; 19:5, Deuteronomy 7:6; 14:2; 26:18). The idea of the covenant is linked to this (Levit-

7 Elwell, W. A., & Beitzel, B. J. (1988). *Church*. In Baker encyclopedia of the Bible (Vol. 1, pp. 458–461). Grand Rapids, MI: Baker Book House.

icus 26:9-12). In the preaching of the prophets, where the judgment of God is often seen as leading to complete destruction, there is also the vision of the reestablishment and re-creation of the people of God (Jeremiah 32:37-38, Hosea 2:1, 23, Ezekiel 11:20; 36:28). In the development of Judaism after the exile, the idea emerges that it is only the Israel of the future, the final Messianic community, which will be "people of God" in the full sense of that term.

It is evident from a number of passages in the Newer Testament that the church knew itself to be these future people of God. The clearest passage is 1 Peter 2:9, "You are a chosen race, a royal priesthood, a holy nation, God's own people." The expressions "royal priesthood" and "holy nation" are taken from Exodus 19:6, which so powerfully expresses both the participation in God's reign and the priestly service of the people of God in the world. Just as the original people of God were called to proclaim God's mighty acts of deliverance (Isaiah 43:20-21, Greek Older Testament), so the new people of God are called to "declare the wonderful deeds of him who called you out of darkness into his marvelous light" (1 Peter 2:9). Hosea 2:1, 23 is cited as support for the contention that the Christian community is the new people of God (Romans 9:25-26, 1 Peter 2:10).

The church is only the church collectively, not individually. We are not known by our individual selves but by our corporate selves. Therefore, it is vital that the church participates in physical gatherings. When the church can't gather, as in the case of the exile and persecution, it was almost impossible to execute the mission of the covenant. We are God's people, and we are called together worldwide as a witness of His presence among His people and to hear instructions for holy living from those who have been called and had a burning bush experience.

The Church in Physical Gathering in House to House
When we look at the inception of the Newer Testament church, we discover that physical gathering was in the DNA of the disciples and the early church. Physical gathering was organic among the people of God. Thus, we have the disciples and believers in the early church attending Temple services daily. When the church was birthed on Pentecost, the church began to have its own gathering separate from its Temple gatherings. The distinction in gathering was based upon covenants, doctrine, and mission. The disciples still saw themselves as a part of Judaism and the Jewish community; thus, they went to the Temple and gathered as a matter of custom and right. However, because of the Jewish resistance to Christ, they had to have their own meetings, not in synagogues, but in their houses, to share the teachings of Jesus and the Kingdom of God. Gathering was such a part of the religious culture and mandate that the disciples continued in the Temple and the house (Acts 2:46).

Physical gathering is a part of the covenant with Christ; we are God's people, not "person." The strength of the early church in exercising the mission of the church was physical gathering, which we find throughout the early church and the Jewish diaspora. The church of Jesus Christ physically gathers; there is no church without physical gathering. Thus, Paul wrote that Christ has placed these in the church, first apostles, second prophets, third teachers... (1 Corinthians 12:28). He stated that the church is the ground and pillar of truth (1 Timothy 3:15); it is where the people of God gather around the Word of God in the embassy of the Kingdom.

You cannot have a Newer Testament church without the concept of physical gathering. Physical gathering is our witness to the world. If you are looking for God, you should be able to find Him in the house of God among the people of God who have come together in His name. God promised to be in the midst of physical gathering (Matthew 18:20). But like in Temple worship, there must be appropriate leadership protocols present. For example, just like there must be a *minyan* in the synagogue to be considered an official gathering, there must be fivefold ministry gifts or their appointees to be an official gathering of the church

To sum up the role and function of the church as the gathering institution of God among the nations, let's summarize the role of the church:

1. Those who have been called into community (*ekklesia*)

2. The new mediatorial agents of the Kingdom (those who have been given the keys to the Kingdom, which represents evangelism and discipleship) – Matthew 16:18-19

3. The embassy of the Kingdom (the place of con-flict resolution and the pillar and ground of truth) – Matthew 18:17, 1 Timothy 3:15

4. The community of the Spirit – Acts 1:8, Luke 24:48

5. The conduit of grace and the temples of the Holy Spirit – 1 Corinthians 6:19

6. The Body of Christ – Ephesians 1:22-23, 1 Corinthians 12

7. The Bride of Christ – Ephesians 5:22

We are a:

- Chosen race (γένος ἐκλεκτόν)

- Royal priesthood (βασίλειον ἱεράτευμα)

- Holy nation (ἔθνος ἅγιος)

- God's own (purchased) people (λαὸς εἰς περιποίησιν)

The Newer Testament church is a living organism that gathers as the people of God with protocols repre-senting the Kingdom of God's governmental structure so that things may be decent and in order. The church cannot be the church unless it is in physical gather-ing, based on the etymology of the word "church" and its Hebrew counterpart, qahal. The terms ekklesia and qahal are terms of assembly.

The Church in Physical Gathering in Eschatology
Through biblical examples and scriptural endorse-ment, we have discussed and demonstrated the sig-nificance of physical gathering as the order of God. Therefore, we must understand that physical gather-ing is not an option. It is the means of identifying who we are, as the Body of Christ, the Church of the Living

God, assembled together with every joint supplying. There is no such concept of the individual being the church. The church is only the church when gathered with apostolic leadership present, just like the synagogue could not officially meet until a minyan (10 men) was present to officiate the synagogue gathering.

Eldridge Street Synagogue, New York City, USA

When we consider the concept of the church, which we have explored in great detail, from both a language and historical perspective, we know that both Israel and the church represent a community that represents God, not an individual. Even when we consider the gathering and eschatology or end-time issues, we examine the seven churches of Asia Minor. When Jesus gave His commendations and condemnations, they were issued to the churches as a whole, not any particular individual. In particular, to the church of Laodicea, Jesus stood on the outside of the church door, knocking and calling for individuals who could still hear His voice amidst the carnal and secular spirit of Laodicea that took over the Spirit of Christ (Revelation 3:14-22). Christ's call was come out from among them, insinuating them to go to the Remnant Church.

The call to come out is both an existential and an eschatological call. This suggests that during this church age, Christ is calling those who are a part of the invisible church to come out from among those who are simply a part of the visible church. It is not clear whether or not this call is exclusively taking place during the church age, or if the knock specifically precedes the rapture or the great snatch of the church, mentioned in 1 Thessalonians 4:13-18:

> *Now, brothers, we want you to know the truth about those who have died; otherwise, you might become sad the way other people do who have nothing to hope for. For since we believe that Yeshua died and rose again, we also believe that in the same way God, through Yeshua, will take with him those who have died. When we say this, we base it on the Lord's own word: we who remain alive when the Lord comes will certainly not take precedence over those who have died. For the Lord himself will come down from heaven with a rousing cry, with a call from one of the ruling angels, and with God's shofar; those who died united with the Messiah will be the first to rise; then we who are left still alive will be caught up with them in the clouds to meet the Lord in the air; and thus we will always be with the Lord. So encourage each other with these words.*

Paul explained that the archangel of the Lord will blow the shofar or trumpet, which is a call or summons to the church to come out of the world. We refer to this experience as "the rapture," which is preceded by the descension of Christ in the clouds, the blowing of the trumpet, and the dead in Christ rising first. Even the resurrection of the dead, when the spirits of individuals who have been with the Lord will be reunited with their physical bodies, is a corporate gathering, not simply an individual gathering. This is what Paul stated will happen in glorification, when the mortal puts on immortality. Paul wrote the following in 1 Corinthians 15:50-58:

> *"Let me say this, brothers: flesh and blood cannot share in the Kingdom of God, nor can something that decays share in what does not decay. Look, I will tell you a secret — not all of us will die! But we will all be changed! It will take but a moment, the blink of an eye, at the final shofar. For the shofar will sound, and the dead will be raised to live forever, and we too will be changed. For this material which can decay must be clothed with imperishability, this which is mortal must be clothed with immortality. When what decays puts on imperishability and what is mortal puts on immortality, then this passage in the Tanakh will be fulfilled:*
>
> *"Death is swallowed up in victory.*
> *"Death, where is your victory?*
> *Death, where is your sting?"*
>
> *The sting of death is sin; and sin draws its power from the Torah; but thanks be to God, who gives us the victory through our Lord Yeshua the Messiah! So, my dear brothers, stand firm and immovable, always doing the Lord's work as vigorously as you can, knowing that united with the Lord your efforts are not in vain.*

The rapture of the church is a corporate event, not an individual event. The trumpet is calling for the invisible church or the elect of God, those who have been born again, not simply attending church but active parts and joints in the Body of Christ. While the term "rapture" does not appear in the scripture, the literal word used in the Greek text is ἁρπάζω (*harpazó*), which means "to snatch away, take away, seize." Some translators just translate *harpazó* (ἁρπάζω) as "rapture." But the Greek text states that the great snatch is a corporate event, not an individual event. Thus, the text says that "we," who are alive, will be caught up or "snatched together" "with them" in the clouds to meet the Lord in the air. There shall "we" always be with the Lord. The end of the church age culminates with a corporate gathering of the invisible church of the elect who are a part of the visible church.

apud: phillip medhurst   THE RAPTURE: ONE IN THE BED. LUKE 17:34. JAN LUYKEN   excudit: harry kossuth

It is vitally important that we began to think and hope with biblical expectation, a corporate hope, not simply an individual hope. We comfort one another with corporate hope. Even after the church age, which exists from Pentecost to the rapture or great snatch, we are called to a gathering in eschatology. We are called to the corporate gathering of the Bema, the judgment of believers (2 Corinthians 5:9-11). After the rapture of the church, we find no focus on the individual. The book of Revelation speaks of a number that no man can number (Revelation 7:9). Thus, all we see in the book of Revelation is corporate gathering. From the evaluation of the seven churches (not the seven individuals) to the people around the throne of God, numerous references attest to the multiplicity of people who will be corporately gathered around or before the throne of God (Revelation 1-4).

The eternal Kingdom of God is a place of corporate gathering. Heaven is not a place where individuals reside as a representation of themselves, but every individual represents the King of Glory. We all are reflections of Him just as the angels corporately gather and reflect His glory, not their agenda. The church and Israel will be gathered together in the eschaton, the 12 tribes and the 12 apostles, representing the church and Israel corporately gathered as the people of God.

6 THE VISIBLE AND THE INVISIBLE CHURCH

We have established that the church is called to physical gatherings from its etymological roots. The church is a gathering institution, and without gathering, there is no church. The church is a sacred assembly – the people of God are called to represent God and His Kingdom among the nations. In our contemporary church, people have erroneously argued that they, as individuals, are the church. However, the church is the assembly and operates under the governmental structure of Kingdom representatives with its fivefold ministry gifts. The church is the physical expression of God as the ground and pillar of truth. Unfortunately, no individual represents the church alone; we are the church we gather, not as individuals. This argument is forged not to feel obligated to the local church, for if I am the church, wherever I am is the church. The Bible doesn't teach this concerning the church; the local church is an assembly of the saints.

The church is the physical and spiritual representation of God on earth. When we look at the historical traditions of the church, we discover a lot about the significance of the physical gathering. The church has been a physical gathering since its origin in the book of Acts; from house to house, they gathered. The Bible states that the Lord added to the church daily those who were being saved. God physically added people to the Messianic community, the assembly and gathering, better known as the church. The church was able to count the number of those who were added to the church – on one occasion, 3,000 were added; on another, 5,000 men alone (Acts 2:41; 4:4). This was possible because the church physically gathered. The early church held each other accountable in physical worship and assembly.

It was the custom of the early church to gather; this is how the apostles met with the churches from city to city and town to town. They witnessed of the resurrection in the synagogue and Temple. The early church did not possess formal assembly halls or physical structures; thus, they gathered in people's homes. Before the Jewish diaspora and persecution, Christ's followers were allowed to meet in their homes, though with Jewish opposition. After the diaspora or Jewish persecution by the Romans, they were no longer able to gather, for they were being hunted, imprisoned, and executed because of their faith in Christ. During the persecution of the church, the Christians were not freely allowed to gather because the Roman guards would arrest them and bring them to "so-called" Roman justice for the fire that destroyed Rome.

What many contemporary believers fail to realize is that the early church met in the perils of death. For over two centuries, the Christ-followers were openly put to death by being rolled down mountainsides in spiked barrels, fed to hungry lions in the Roman colosseums, and wrapped in pitch and burned as torches in the colosseums and streets. Even though gathering would often cost their lives, the church still gathered regardless of the possible consequences. Physical gathering put their lives in danger, but they understood the significance of maintaining their witness and walk with Christ, which included physical gatherings. The church would secretly gather in catacombs or mountainside caves to not be noticed by the Roman guards. The church understood they were not the church unless they gathered. The church is an apostolic assembly that convenes in a physical gathering. The church physically gathered in secret to continue to hear the Word of God and to be encouraged to stand firm amid opposition.

An Eastern Roman mosaic showing a basilica with towers, mounted with Christian crosses

The early church gathered and the church in the diaspora gathered during the persecution by the Romans. After the persecution of the church ceased through the signings of the Edict of Milan and the Edict of Toleration, which stopped Christian persecution, they were able to physically gather without consequence. When persecution ceased, one of the first rules of order was to establish the principle of gathering. As the new and official religion of Rome through Constantine the Great, Christians were provided with physical structures referred to as basilicas or Christian churches. Thus, the church was allowed to gather without the threat of death openly and physically. During this era, the Patristic Period, the early church fathers began working on interpreting scripture and church creeds for the gathered church. Just as Israel gathered, the church gathered, for the church is a physically gathering community. The church's ecclesiastical doctrine was being developed by early church fathers for hundreds of years.

The Emperor Constantine, accompanied by the bishops of the First Council of Nicaea (325), holding the Niceno-Constantinopolitan Creed of 381

Our history is riddled with churches that have strayed from the purpose of the church. One of the early church fathers, St. Augustine of Hippo, who provided the church with immeasurable jewels of biblical interpretations, wrote about the church's role in the world. In his book, *The City of God*, he wrote about the visible and the invisible church. I believe that a look at Augustine's thesis on the distinction between the invisible and the visible church is pertinent to the discussion of the church and physical gathering. The Nicene Creed demonstrates how important the church was and is to the existence of what we refer to today as Christianity stating, "the one holy catholic and apostolic church." Augustine posited that there is a distinction between the visible and invisible church. So let's take a deeper dive into his theological construct.

The invisible church or church invisible is a theological concept of an "invisible" Christian church of the elect who are known only to God. The invisible church stands in contrast to the "visible church"—that is, the institutional body on earth, which preaches the gospel and administers the sacraments, which in Protestantism, we refer to as ordinances or the Lord's Supper. Every member of the invisible church is saved. In contrast, the visible church contains some individuals who are saved and others who are unsaved. The following Bible verses speak of the distinction between the visible church and the invisible church and were used to build this argument:[1]

> "Not everyone who says to me, 'Lord, Lord!' will enter the Kingdom of Heaven, only those who do what my Father in heaven wants. On that Day, many will say to me, 'Lord, Lord! Didn't we prophesy in your name? Didn't we expel demons in your name? Didn't we perform many miracles in your name?' Then I will tell them to their faces, 'I never knew you! Get away from me, you workers of lawlessness!' So, everyone who hears these words of mine and acts on them will be like a sensible man who built his house on bedrock. The rain fell, the rivers flooded, the winds blew and beat against that house, but it didn't collapse, because its foundation was on rock. But everyone who hears these words of mine and does not act on them will be like a stupid

1 Wikipedia. Church Invisible, Retrieved from https://en.wikipedia.org/wiki/Invisible_church

man who built his house on sand. The rain fell, the rivers flooded, the wind blew and beat against that house, and it collapsed — and its collapse was horrendous!" – Matthew 7:21-27

Yeshua put before them another parable. "The Kingdom of Heaven is like a man who sowed good seed in his field; but while people were sleeping, his enemy came and sowed weeds among the wheat, then went away. When the wheat sprouted and formed heads of grain, the weeds also appeared. The owner's servants came to him and said, 'Sir didn't you sow good seed in your field? Where have the weeds come from?' He answered, 'An enemy has done this.' The servants asked him, 'Then do you want us to go and pull them up?' But he said, 'No, because if you pull up the weeds, you might uproot some of the wheat at the same time. Let them both grow together until the harvest; and at harvest-time I will tell the reapers to collect the weeds first and tie them in bundles to be burned, but to gather the wheat into my barn.'" – Matthew 13:24-30

"But immediately following the trouble of those times, the sun will grow dark, the moon will stop shining, the stars will fall from the sky, and the powers in heaven will be shaken. Then the sign of the Son of Man will appear in the sky, all the tribes of the Land will mourn, and they will see the Son of Man coming on the clouds of heaven with tremendous power and glory. He will send out his angels with a great shofar; and they will gather together

his chosen people from the four winds, from one end of heaven to the other. Now let the fig tree teach you its lesson: when its branches begin to sprout and leaves appear, you know that summer is approaching. In the same way, when you see all these things, you are to know that the time is near, right at the door. Yes! I tell you that this people will certainly not pass away before all these things happen. Heaven and earth will pass away, but my words will never pass away.

"But when that day and hour will come, no one knows — not the angels in heaven, not the Son, only the Father. For the Son of Man's coming will be just as it was in the days of Noach. Back then, before the Flood, people went on eating and drinking, taking wives and becoming wives, right up till the day Noach entered the ark; and they didn't know what was happening until the Flood came and swept them all away. It will be just like that when the Son of Man comes. Then there will be two men in a field — one will be taken and the other left behind. There will be two women grinding flour at the mill — one will be taken and the other left behind. So stay alert, because you don't know on what day your Lord will come. But you do know this: had the owner of the house known when the thief was coming, he would have stayed awake and not allowed his house to be broken into. Therefore you too must always be ready, for the Son of Man will come when you are not expecting him. Who is the faithful and sensible servant whose master puts him in charge of the household staff, to give them

their food at the proper time? It will go well with that servant if he is found doing his job when his master comes. Yes, I tell you that he will put him in charge of all he owns. But if that servant is wicked and says to himself, 'My master is taking his time'; and he starts beating up his fellow servants and spends his time eating and drinking with drunkards; then his master will come on a day the servant does not expect, at a time he doesn't know; and he will cut him in two and put him with the hypocrites, where people will wail and grind their teeth! – Matthew 24:29-51

St. Augustine was inspired to use this construct as part of his refutation of the Donatist sect. Who were the Donatists? Members of a schismatic Christian group in North Africa, formed in 311AD, believed that only those living a blameless life belonged in the church. They ceased to exist in the 7th century. It is believed that Augustine was strongly influenced by the Platonist belief that true reality is invisible. However, if the visible reflects the invisible, it does so only partially and imperfectly. The concept of visi-

The earliest known portrait of Saint Augustine in a 6th-century fresco, Lateran, Rome

ble and invisible church was strongly used during the Protestant Reformation to distinguish between the "visible" Roman Catholic Church, which according to the Reformers was corrupt, and those within who truly believe, as well as true believers within their own denominations.[2]

2 Ibid

John Calvin described the invisible church as "that which is actually in God's presence, into which no persons are received but those who are children of God by the grace of adoption and true members of Christ through sanctification of the Holy Spirit." The invisible church includes not only the saints presently living on earth but all the elect from the beginning of the world." He continued in contrasting this church with the church scattered throughout the world. "In this church, there is a very large mixture of hypocrites, who have nothing of Christ but the name and outward appearance..." (Institutes 4.1.7).[3]

In the 17th century, Pietism, an influential religious reform movement among German Lutherans that emphasized personal faith against the main Lutheran church's perceived stress on doctrine and theology over Christian living, emerged.[4] As the discussion of the visible church and invisible church continued, Pietism later took things a step further with its formulation of *ecclesiolae* in the ecclesia ("little churches within the church").[5]

> "Roman Catholic theology, reacting against the Protestant concept of an invisible Church, emphasized the visible aspect of the Church founded by Christ, but in the twentieth century placed more stress on the interior life of the Church as a supernatural organism, identifying the Church, as in the encyclical Mystici corporis Christi of Pope Pius XII, with the Mystical Body of Christ."[6]

---

3 Ibid.
4 Britannica. *Pietism*, Retrieved from https://www.britannica.com/topic/Pietism
5 Wikipedia, *Church Invisible*.
6 Ibid

In Catholic doctrine, the one true Church is the visible society founded by Christ, namely, the Catholic Church under the global jurisdiction of the bishop of Rome. However, the Roman Catholic Church rejected the idea of the church as a rationalistic or purely sociological vs. a merely human organization with structures and activities. The visible church and its structures exist, but the church is more, as it is guided by the Holy Spirit.[7] The Roman Catholic Church also rejected the idea that the Church is an exclusive mystical (invisible) church, though it fully embraces the church's union with Christ at all times – "Christ in us." However, "Christ in us" does not deify the church members though the church has a supernatural end.

The concept of the visible and invisible church has been pondered by the Patristics, Roman Catholics, Reformers, and modern-day theologians on a quest for the true identity of the church. From the scriptures, it is clear that everyone who names the name of Christ is not a part of the church due to the lack of authenticity of their confession of faith. Even the scriptures state that not everyone who says unto God, "Lord, Lord" will enter the Kingdom of heaven (Matthew 7:21). Thus, as we attempt to understand the church and the significance of gathering, we acknowledge that throughout history, the fact that we gather doesn't mean that we are a part of Christ's true church. Not everyone who attends church services is a part of the church, and the visible church is distinct from the invisible. The visible church differs from the invisible church in nature and function, but not in purpose. While the visible church strives to represent the Christian message, it will, by its nature, consistently fail to do so completely and must be treated like any other imperfect human organiza-

---

7 Ibid

tion.[8] The church is full of people who are being transformed through the process of sanctification.

The invisible church is a term for all believers in Jesus Christ throughout history. Humans cannot fully discern belief, an internal feeling; only God can discern the invisible church's membership. The invisible church is a purely spiritual organization, bound together by God, and described by Paul as "we, though many, are one body." The members of the invisible church believe in Jesus Christ, have died to themselves, and subjected themselves to the Lordship of Christ the Savior. This belief is more than mere mental assent. We use it in contemporary language; it denotes trust, loyalty, and reliance. One who believes in Jesus Christ follows His teachings and lives in His stead; He died for us; therefore, we live for Him.[9]

A visible church is a human organization that supports Christians in their varied expressions of belief and trust in Christ. Like other human organizations, the visible church members define the organization by external actions, such as attending worship services and, some-

8 Augustine Collective. *The Visible and Invisible Church*, Retrieved from http://augustinecollective.org/visible-invisible-church/
9 Ibid.

times, by formal requirements. The members of a visible church meet, communicate, and work together to pursue common goals. A visible church is often instituted under secular law and establishes an internal government. Typically, a visible church owns property like any other organization. The visible church gathers in its said property, a secular domain for the expression of faith in Christ in totality. Visible churches support Christians in their belief in Christ in varying ways, such as the Lord's Supper, baptism, weddings, funerals, etc. Even though visible churches vary in supporting Christians, all visible churches can be discussed collectively as the visible church.[10] The visible church includes all the churches who embrace Christ as Lord and Savior through the shared ordinances and evangelism and discipleship. The visible church is and can only be visible in assembly or gathering, or the presence of the church disappears. Steven Lee states:

> "The visible church and the invisible church overlap, but are not coextensive. The Second Vatican Council described this relationship by declaring in 1964 that the invisible church "subsists in the [Roman] Catholic Church." Lutherans extended this to all visible churches. Subsist means "to exist, persist, or continue," and implies a complicated interrelation between the visible and the invisible church. Visible churches provide for the institutional needs of the invisible church, just as a house provides for those who live within. The invisible church also exists outside the visible church. Since the invisible church subsists in, not as, the visible church, nonbelievers may subsist in the visible church. Not all participants in the visible church are members of the invisible church. The weakness of the verb "to subsist"

---

10 Ibid.

indicates that unbelievers may not only subsist in, but may rule and distort the visible church."[11]

What is clear is the fact that the visible church is made up of both those who are in Christ and those who are not in Christ. Thus, in the church, we will have those who corrupt, rebel, and outright revolt against the church, for they are not a part of the elect or the invisible church. Those who are a part of the invisible church WILL GATHER.

Although sometimes distorted, the visible church derives its purpose and belief in Jesus from the invisible church, the church that Jesus built, known as the early church. Christians have long wrestled with describing their belief. In the fourth century, the Second Ecumenical Council adopted the Nicene Creed, which is accepted today by the Roman Catholic, the Eastern Orthodox, and most Protestant churches. The creed presents a broad, helpful, and orthodox understanding of the invisible church. It describes the invisible church as "the one holy catholic and apostolic church." [12]

Apostolic
Explication of the Nicene Creed reveals that while the invisible church is genuinely unified, sanctified, apostolic, and universal, the visible church, a human organization, is none of those things. The two churches share in purpose but differ in nature. The invisible church, subsisting in the visible church, strives to hold the visible church true to its mission.[13]

> "The descriptor apostolic means the invisible church is founded upon the tradition passed down from the twelve disciples. This term de-

11 Ibid.
12 Ibid.
13 Ibid.

scribes how "the household of God" is "built on the foundation of the apostles and prophets," and they on Jesus. The invisible church preaches the message of the apostles, those "sent out," that has been recounted in scripture "from those who from the beginning were eyewitnesses."[14]

Catholic

The next defining term is "catholic." The word "catholic" – Greek καθολικός – means "general or universal." The term "catholic" refers to the span of the invisible church across denominations, cultures, languages, and centuries. The contemporary Protestant theologian, Douglas John Hall, describes the defining belief of the invisible church as "pondered over by centuries of the faithful," hinting at the unifying purpose provided by the invisible church.[15]

One

The term "one" indicates unity in God despite differences in time, place, and teaching. Given the span of the invisible church, this is neither unity of tradition nor organization. For instance, Paul met the other apostles after three years of ministry. Yet, "there is one body and one Spirit, ... one Lord, one faith, one baptism, one God

14 Ibid.
15 Ibid.

and Father of all, who is over all and through all and in all." In other words, the invisible church is unified under one Lord. The rule of this common Lord, as He and the one Spirit guide and direct the invisible church, provides unity of purpose and direction. Indeed, the creed begins with the subject "we," which refers to the invisible church. The confession of belief in "God, the Father almighty," "Jesus Christ, the only Son of God," and "the Holy Spirit" reinforces the unified identity of the invisible church.[16]

Holy
Finally, holy means set apart by God's choosing. The Nicene Creed describes the invisible church as a worldwide body of people, set apart from the ways of the world and of sin by Jesus Christ. The visible church is also set apart from other human organizations to the extent that it represents God and follows the purpose of the invisible church.[17]

Unlike the invisible church, the visible church is not unified, sanctified, apostolic, or universal. It is divided amongst many visible churches that fight each other. Unlike the invisible church, unified and coordinated by Jesus, visible churches rarely act together. This disharmony stems from their human nature. Visible churches consist of people who, in their nature, act sinfully and proclaim themselves rather than God. Although visible churches seek to teach the apostolic message, much of what they teach is derived from traditional and contemporary human culture. Thus, while the visible church seeks to support the invisible church, it can never do so perfectly as a collection of limited human organizations.[18]

---

16 Ibid.
17 Ibid.
18 Ibid.

The Nicene Creed continues to describe the church's purpose with its final statement that "we look for the resurrection of the dead and the life of the world to come." Paul not only expected but sought to "attain the resurrection from the dead." The invisible church lives in confident expectation of the future resurrection and looks for "the life of the world to come." While of the world to come, this life is not found exclusively in the world to come. Across time, the invisible church remembers, "He [the Holy Spirit] will [and does]...grant eternal life to me and to all who believe in Christ."[19]

The final contrast is the "invisible church looks for its preservation into the world to come, while the visible church is fleeting by nature. In heaven, there will be no need for the government or property that is currently needed by the visible church. When not following Jesus, the visible church may pursue its own preservation and turn away from its mission as a house for the eternal, invisible church. Hope binds all the members of the invisible church together and, if remembered,

19 Ibid.

can do the same for the visible church despite its forgetful nature."[20]

While the purpose of both the visible and invisible church is the same, the imperfect, visible church struggles with pressures of the external world, constantly trying to redefine the church's role outside of the Bible. The big challenge is that the church desires what the world desires in many cases, which puts it in the position of Israel and its compromise. The visible church continues to be plagued by racism, sexism, classism, and denominationalism.

Unfortunately, many are aware of the flaws of the visible church in that it is full of both wheat and tare. As a result, it falls terribly short of the standard of Christ at times. However, it is still the church of the invisible church. Despite this flawed human nature, the visible church retains the purpose of the invisible church across the broad sweep of history. However, as flawed as the church may be, Jesus assures us that the invisible church will survive when He states that "on this rock, I will build my church, and the gates of Hades will not overcome it." The invisible church will always subsist in visible churches since Christians, as humans, require social structure to support their faith.[21]

The visible human organization in which the invisible church is housed will always be flawed, lacking perfect unity and holiness, straying from its purpose of supporting Christian belief. For the visible church to maintain its purpose, the invisible church must indwell and guide the visible church.[22] Simply put, the wheat and the tare must grow together, and, at harvest time, God will separate the two. One final note to cite from Au-

20 Ibid.
21 Ibid.
22 Ibid.

gustine is that you can be in the visible church and not a part of the invisible church, but you cannot be a part of the invisible church and not be in the visible church. The church is the church only in gathering. Thus, the church, the ekklesia, is the physical assembly of the saints!

THE WORK OF COMMUNITY (ACTS 4:32-35)

As we examine the biblical tradition of the church and the significance of gathering, it must never be forgotten that the church, as was Israel, is called to both a vertical and horizontal relationship with God and God's people, as declared in the Decalogue or Ten Commandments. God is the God of unity in community!

I believe that it is the intention of God for us to understand the significance of community. In the book of Genesis, God postured Himself as a community God when He referred to Himself as "Us" (Genesis 1:26). In Genesis 1:27, God created humankind, both male and female, which is the foundation for community. Then He commanded them to be fruitful and multiply after their kind; in other words, He commanded humanity to procreate to form a community (Genesis 1:28). While we see God begin with a thinly veiled emphasis on community, He created Adam from the dust of the earth, and then clearly validated that it was not good for man to be alone (Genesis 2:18). Of course, Adam was not really alone, but he did not have a community. He did not share a meaningful relationship with the animals because they were not his equal. And he did not share in the community with the Triune God because he was not Their equal. Thus, God pulled his partner, Eve, from his ribcage, and the two became a nuclear family (Genesis 2:21-24).

Together, they formed a community and became the future hub for communities to come. What made them community was that they were equal in image, they were compatible in fellowship, they were available for communication, and they shared common interests, vision, and values. They had all things in common until the serpent came to kill, steal, and destroy their form of community. He did so using his main strategy of divide and conquer – to put people in isolation from one another. Satan hates community and loves individualism, because God loves community and hates individualism. After God created the path for creation to form communities of every kind, He saw everything that He created, and it was good (Genesis 1:31). Community was in the mind of God but not a reality for humans yet, which suggests that community must be built; it is a developmental process. However, though Satan hates the God-loving community, he was the progenitor of the anti-God community — sinners. Thus, community produces either for God or Satan.

Community is a Kingdom value designed by God to procreate and expand the Kingdom of God. Genesis begins with the design and making of community. Jesus exemplified community. Then the Apostle Paul picked up this same theme and referred to the narrative of Adam and Eve in Ephesians 5 as a paradigm of the church as a community. However, before Paul provided us with the paradigm of Christ and the church and the husband and the wife as the basis of community, he explained the unity of community in Ephesians 4:5-6, stating one Lord, one faith, one baptism, one body, one Father, who is of all, above all, and in all.

The first three chapters of Ephesians are principally doctrine, which unfolds God's redemptive plan and purpose for His creation. Chapter 4 makes a shift from theological to practical – from that which is both fascinating and inspiring to that which moves us to act, "from the believer's wealth in Christ to the believer's walk in Christ." God's new community must now live by a new standard. Paul spoke to the church, not as an individual, but as the Body of Christ. One's beliefs should inform one's behavior; thus, Paul called for the community to put into action what they said they believed. Paul urged the church to move from individual understanding to corporate or community practice. In Paul's writings, it is clear that he was speaking to a gathered people, because they couldn't even have access to his letters except when they gathered.

Paul exhorted the church to live in the unity of community by getting along with each other. He posited that the quarreling was due to what happened when they gathered. Maintaining the spirit of unity and executing the mission of the invisible church of Christ requires humility, meekness (the ability to put up with what God is working on), longsuffering, patience, and diligence in keeping the unity of the community. In the book of Ephesians, Paul teaches us that we have both the call of unity of community and diversity of gifts, which help build the overall community. Thus, a healthy community advances from the unity of community to the diversity of gifts, suggesting the significance of the individual's contribution to the community. The gift is designed to help us; orchestrated and managed by the fivefold ministry gifts, the community is called to the work of ministry. The assignment of the work of ministry is not an independent work but a corporate work that is designed to bring people to Christ the King and the Kingdom of God through His church (Ephesians 4:11-16).

The Apostle Paul declared that Christ is the head of the church, which is His body, "the fullness of Him who fills all in all" (Ephesians 1:22-23). Though Paul calls for the unity of community in Ephesians 4, and really throughout the entire epistle, community seems to be an optional feature of 21st century Christianity. Being connected to the local church and a contributing partner in the contemporary church is thought to be voluntary based upon the desires of the individual. However, when it comes to the Kingdom of God, the two most important doctrines are the doctrine of the cross and the doctrine of the Kingdom. God creates communities, not individuals; the cross did not give birth to individual desires but to community participation (Ephesians 5:32). The cross is the way to the crown or the Kingdom, which is community life. When we give our lives to Christ by way of the cross, we are born again or become a new creation as God's Kingdom citizens. We become a chosen generation, a royal priesthood, a holy nation, God's special people to be possessed by God (1 Peter 2:9). In the book of Revelation, John saw a number that no man could number (Revelation 7:9).

Salvation is a call to community, and community happens through the physical gathering. A Kingdom community, much like other communities, is comprised of people having common interests, a shared vision and values, similar norms and mores, and sharing a common progenitor. Community is a necessity for the development of healthy individuals, who all suffer, in the words of Maslow,  from the need for belonging, which feeds our self-esteem and fuels actualization. The physical gathering of a community outputs healthy individuals. Likewise, the physical gathering of the church produces healthy disciples. Without physical gathering, the church will have limited outputs of Kingdom disciples, if any.

The challenge of community is that people get hurt, and hurt people hurt people. Church hurt is one of the primary reasons people stop attending church. People have offenses with one another or the church's leadership and tend not to approach the conflict through

Kingdom protocols of conflict resolution (Matthew 18:15-20). This is where the Kingdom community differs from other communities. The community of faith is the only community in creation that is empowered by the Holy Spirit. The Holy Spirit is there to help us get along with one another because, by nature, we can all be community terrorists. Without physical gathering, believers will not recognize where they are in their walk with God and will simply approach their walk with God subjectively.

In Acts 4:32-35, Paul provides us with some compelling truths and tips that can help us build community, make an impact upon the world, and transform each person within the community by the power of the Holy Spirit. People resist community because community requires humility, obedience, submission, sacrifice, denial, and maturity. Community is work; it is not a passive development. Community means living through the cross with other believers with the aspiration of entering the eternal Kingdom. Paul stated that we must all enter the Kingdom through much tribulation (Acts 14:22).

I believe that while some of the tribulations are due to external forces, most of the tribulationa are an inside job. Most likely, tribulations come from people's inability to walk in the fruit of the Spirit and be patient and loving with one another. Since I've been saved, it has not been the sinners who have hurt and hindered me; it has been the church members, the so-called members of the Kingdom community. However, as I have always mentioned, I'd rather live in the mess of the ark (Noah's Ark) than die in the flood. Hence, you must learn to let it go and walk it off, not out of pride but out of an understanding that you do the same things to others and God. We must never forget that none of us are, to date, what we will be when God completes us. Therefore, we must be patient with one another and have the desire to physically gather.

The enemy tries to make us think that it is much easier to live for God in isolation or around a few select people rather than come to the physical gathering of the church. But when we meet in the sacred gathering of the church, there is an anointing that flows from Aaron's beard down to the body. To ignore the structure of community is to ignore God. Christ built His movement in community; the Newer Testament church was built through community, from the Temple to the house. And Jesus declared that He is present in community, "For wherever two or three are assembled in my name, I am there with them" (Matthew 18:20).

The local church provides us with the power of community, and the Bible declares that community is the methodology for people to co-exist with shared vision and values based upon apostolic teaching and preaching. Luke declares the following, in Acts 4:32-35, about the early church and community:

1. Community is built upon integration

All the many believers were one in heart and soul, and no one claimed any of his possessions for himself... – Acts 4:32

The early church thought in terms of community, so no one considered anything they had as their own, for they had all things in common (v. 32). The Greek word for "common" is κοινός (*koinós*), which means "that which is common to all or belonging to all." Not only does the same Spirit that raised Christ from the dead give life to our mortal bodies, but the same Spirit integrates us into the Body of Christ. The text teaches us about the power of integration. Christianity is the community of the integrated. We are integrated into the Body of Christ. Paul writes, "For just as the body is one but has many parts; and all the parts of the body, though many, constitute one body; so it is with the Messiah. For it was by one Spirit that we were all immersed into one body, whether Jews or Gentiles, slaves or free; and we were all given the one Spirit to drink" (1 Corinthians 12:12-13, CJB). Being a believer is about being integrated into the body, but to be integrated into the body, you must lose yourself. Jesus said, "He that loses his life will save it." (Mark 8:35). The individual must physically gather with the visible church if, in fact, they are a part of the invisible church.

2. One must be involved in the community

...but everyone shared everything he had. – *Acts 4:32b*

Their heart and soul were into the vision of the church; there was a necessity of involvement. Thus, they did everything they possibly could to bring the vision of Christ to pass: knowing Him, making Him known to others, and spreading the Kingdom message around the globe through multiple vehicles (v. 32). No one said that anything was their own. The Greek word for "own" is ἴδιος (*idios*), which means "pertaining to a private person not public." Paul wrote that those who are a part of the community of faith are contributors to the vision through small groups saying, "Under his control, the whole body is being fitted and held together by the support of every joint, with each part working to fulfill its function; this is how the body grows and builds itself up in love" (Ephesians 4:16).

Paul stated in Colossians 2:19 that for a ministry to grow, it must hold fast to the Head and be properly knitted together and nourished by what every joint and ligament supplies, which grows with the increase from God.

- The Greek word for "knitted together" is συμβιβάζω (*sumbibázō*). This word comes from two Greek words – *sun*, meaning "together," and *bibazo*, meaning "to uplift, exalt." Thus, *sumbibázo* means "to cause to come together, join, unite, knit."
- The Greek word for "grows" is αὐξάνω (*auxánō*), which means "to grow, increase, augment, to add to something, grow." This growth comes from elements outside of one's self and includes one's effort of exertion.
- The Greek word for "increate" is αὔξησις (*auxesis*), which means "to grow, growth, increase applied spiritually only, that which comes strictly from God."

- The Greek word for "God" is θεός (Theou), which means "the Godhead, Trinity."

Not only must the church operate in the unity of community, but it also takes an entire church community to exercise the mission of God.

3. Community merits an infusion of great power and great grace

With great power the emissaries continued testifying to the resurrection of the Lord Yeshua, and they were all held in high regard.
– Acts 4:33

Luke wrote that the apostles consistently testified of the resurrection of Jesus with great power. The Greek word for "great" is μέγας (*megas*), meaning "large capacity or magnitude." The Greek word for "power" is δύναμις (*dunamis*), meaning "ability to achieve, ability to be capable; to witness to the resurrection of the Lord Jesus, demonstration of power." And as a result of them preaching with great power, great grace or high regard was given to everyone. The Greek word for "grace" is χάρις (*charis*), meaning "that which causes joy or one to rejoice." The word charis speaks of unmerited favor without expectation of return; absolutely free expression of the loving kindness of God, finding its benevolence and motivation in the heart of the giver.

4. Community involves Kingdom investment

Nor was there anyone among them who lacked; for all who were possessors of lands or houses sold them, and brought the proceeds of the things that were sold... – Acts 4:34

Those who had houses and lands, sold them (liquidated), and brought the proceeds of the things sold. The Greek word for "proceeds" is τιμή (*timé*), which means "to pay honor, respect, value to the apostles." Their seeds made it possible for you and me to be saved; they sponsored the spread of the gospel of the Kingdom. Unfortunately, this is one of the reasons why many don't attend physical gatherings – they do not understand the concept or necessity of community giving.

5. Community sacrifice leads to increase

...and laid them at the apostles' feet; and they distributed to each as anyone had need. – Acts 4:35

As a result of their giving, there was no lack among them. The apostles distributed or empowered the people to prosper. They met the need of the church community through empowerment, not enablement. The Greek word for "need" is χρῆμα (*chréma*), meaning "to use or to be useful, money, business, matter, thing, not a seed." The apostles engaged in cooperative economics and wealth creation. Consider the outcomes of the Jewish people; they were not beggars. Increase, however, is based upon value, not money; seeds sown, not money given. They thought about their giving in terms of business as a seed of support. They brought value and money for the sustainability of the community – the people and the apostles. When the church assembly meets, we meet and sow seeds for the sake of ministry execution, and, as a result, all things will be added to us! When we give, God promises to give back to us – pressed down, shaken together, running over, and we will not have room enough to receive it (Luke 6:38). God will bless your children, your health, your businesses, your career, etc., in physical gathering when you sow, just as Israel did!

The church is a community that is marked by unity. It is the assembly of the saints that physically gather to represent God physically and spiritually on earth. Both Paul and Luke provide a powerful hermeneutic for the church as community and in physical gathering. Paul focused upon the unity of community – one Lord, one faith, one baptism, one body, one Father who is of all, above all and in all (Ephesians 4:5). He also declares that the church community is subject to the fivefold ministry gifts of apostles, prophets, evangelists, pastors, and teachers responsible for equipping the community. Thus, without physical gathering, the church cannot be equipped for the work of ministry.

Without the church leadership, the members of the church cannot complete their assignment. The apostolic leaders are called to manage the community, equip them for the work of ministry, and help them grow into the full stature of Christ so that they will not be tossed to and fro by every wind of doctrine (Ephesians 4:11-14). The apostolic gifts ensure that every joint or member of the body is doing their part and sharing their load. Paul spoke very clearly about the significance of the individual's contribution to the community. Paul's letter to the Ephesians (in Chapter 4) speaks of the diversity of giftings among the laity to contribute to the whole of the church.

Then Paul contrasted the old man and the new man, and he admonishes us to take off the old man with its old nature, be renewed in the spirit of our minds, and put on the new man (Ephesians 4:22-24). The old man doesn't want to gather with the new creations in Christ because his urges and appetites are in contrast with the new man. The new man is connected to the invisible church and desires to please God.

Paul provided the following actions for the building of community and a consistent lifestyle in God:

1. Put off falsehood

> *Therefore, stripping off falsehood, let everyone speak truth with his neighbor, because we are intimately related to each other as parts of a body. – Ephesians 4:25*

The Greek word for "put off" is ἀποτίθημι (*apotithémi*), which means "to lay aside, renounce, lay down." The Greek word for "falsehood" is ψεῦδος (*pseudos*), meaning "making a lie, fictitious embellishment." In other words, Paul was saying to stop lying! Before you communicate anything, you should ask yourself the following questions: Did I see what happened? Did I hear what was said? Do I know the context of the situation? Did the other person get to give you their perspective? Was it in the presence of two witnesses? If the answer is no to all of these, just know that when you repeat what you've heard from someone else, it's a lie! We cannot have community as long as you keep communicating what you heard and not what you saw. It is not godly to speak negatively of people, especially if you're just communicating what you heard from someone else. Whenever you repeat something you were not there to contextually witness, you're destroying community by spreading lies. That's why the scripture says do not receive an accusation against an elder unless it was witnessed by two or three people (1 Timothy 5:19). By necessitating the corroboration of community, God teaches us that our individual warped minds could make the wrong interpretation.

Is this important? Yes! Not lying is so crucial that when God gave Moses the Ten Commandments, one of the laws stated you should not bear false witness (Exodus 20:16). If you don't contextually witness something for yourself, then you have no business talking about it. Just imagine all the lies you've spread about other people by simply telling others what you heard, not what you witnessed. Lying is so repulsive to God that He said He hates a lying tongue (Proverbs 6:17). The Bible says there's a special compartment in eternal judgment that's reserved just for liars – the lake of fire, which burns with fire and brimstone (Revelation 21:8). Do you know how many people's reputations have been destroyed because of lies? Do you know how many people's families have been destroyed because of lies? Do you know how many people's careers have been destroyed because of lies? Lies destroy the community!

So Paul said instead of telling lies, we ought to speak the truth to our neighbor. "Speak" is the Greek term λαλέω (*laleó*), which means "to talk at random." "Truth" in the Greek is ἀλήθεια (*alétheia*), meaning "the reality." "Neighbor" is the Greek term πλησίον (*plésíon*), which means "he that is close by, near." Paul admonishes us to speak truth to all who are close by because even liars talk to anybody who's near them or will hear them. Then Paul tells us why we should speak truth to our neighbors – because we are intimately related to each other as parts of the same body. This is why we don't lie on each other; we tell the truth or speak the truth in love (Ephesians 4:15). Even in the court system, a person is presumed innocent until proven guilty. And to be proven guilty, they have to go through forensics and a host of other things. But for many, all we have to do is hear something about someone, and we think they're guilty. Paul said we should not do this; we are intimately related to each other as parts of the same body. We belong to each other, depend upon each other, and are held together in a covenant relationship that calls for mutual transparency. This epistle is written to people who physically gathered and shared community life together.

2. Stabilize your anger

> *Be angry, but don't sin — don't let the sun go down before you have dealt with the cause of your anger; otherwise you leave room for the Adversary. – Ephesians 4:26-26*

The next thing Paul tells us to do is stabilize our anger. Let me tell you something about me and my anger. I've worked myself up in my mind before, and I've thought certain things, and I've gotten angry. But when I investigated the situation, it was nothing like I thought it was. So I ended up going through all of that anger for nothing. Many times, we work ourselves up in anger because of the narrative we tell ourselves. In Greek, the word "anger" is ὀργίζω (*orgízo*), meaning "wrath, provoked." Paul said to be provoked and have wrath, but do not sin, which means it's okay to become angry.

Anger is a normal part of being human. The Bible talks about the wrath of the Lord. Jesus wasn't happy when He beat the moneychangers out of the Temple (John 2:14-17). As He drove the moneychangers, the oxen, and sheep out of the Temple, turning over tables, He yelled, "Get these things out of here! How dare you turn my Father's house into a market?" Jesus clearly wasn't happy when He did this. He was angry! But the

Bible tells us that even though He was angry, He did not sin (1 Peter 2:22, 2 Corinthians 5:21). Anger is natural. Some people think that every time they see someone get angry that they're sinning, but they're not. There is something called "righteous indignation." I will often take a strong position and show great emotion when I'm preaching, but it's not because I'm angry. I'm just passionate about God and His Word.

Paul then tells us why we shouldn't hold on to our anger overnight – because it gives place to the devil. The Greek word for "devil" here is διάβολος (*diabolos*), which means "to accuse, a false accuser, he who divides people without any reason." So, when you go to bed, close your eyes, and go to sleep without resolving your anger, your mind is still working, even though your physical body has shut down. Your emotions and your mind are unguarded by your consciousness, so Satan gets in your mind, and he makes things worse. When you wake up the next day, you're worse than you were the first day. Why? Because you didn't deal with your anger, and you gave place to the devil. While you were asleep, the devil brought all kinds of stuff to you about the person who angered you. When you don't deal with your anger, the person you are angry with will become much more repulsive the next day. And every day you don't deal with it, they become more repulsive daily until you get to the point where you say, "I hate them!"

What admonishment does Paul give to replace our anger? Paul said, "Be angry, but do not sin," or do not hold on to your anger. As a pastor for many, many years, one of the things I've come to notice about people is that some people have a problem with other people getting angry. Still, those same people will not follow the Bible when it comes to resolving anger. Paul tells us that we shouldn't let the sun go down on our wrath or anger, which means we are supposed to resolve the issues that have caused us to become angry that day. When you don't resolve your anger issues each day, you help to deteriorate the community.

If someone makes you angry today, you cannot tell them you will call them tomorrow to resolve it. Now, it's okay to take some time to get yourself together, but before the day is gone, God expects you to resolve the issue that made you angry. Much of the disunity we experience in the church is because of people who went days, months, and even years without resolving their issues with other people. Much of the disunity you experience in your life is because of the issues you didn't settle with your mom, dad, friends, etc., from the hurt you experienced years ago. So what are you to do? Paul said, let go of your anger and walk it off.

3. Cease from stealing

> *The thief must stop stealing; instead, he should make an honest living by his own efforts. This way he will be able to share with those in need. – Ephesians 4:28*

The third thing Paul tells us to do is cease stealing. Now, I know you may be thinking, "What was going on in Ephesus that made Paul give them this kind of instruction?" Nothing wrong was going on in the church in Ephesus. Paul was just writing to the church through the inspiration of the Holy Spirit. And knowing how human nature works, he knew the types of behaviors that would divide a community. So he said stop stealing. The Greek word for "steal" is κλέπτω (*klépto*), meaning "to steal, cheat, deceive, embezzle." Thus, Paul was saying, "Don't come into the church community with your schemes." Paul said you are not to steal, cheat, deceive, or embezzle the people in the church community; the church community is not for that. The church community is also not the place where you bring your money-building pyramids like selling solar energy, phone cards, insurance, etc. Now, it's okay to do that kind of selling outside of the church, but you cannot exploit the church with your money-making ventures. Paul said this because there are always people who see the masses of people in the church and then dream and calculate how much money they, and possibly the church, could make if they were allowed to sell their product or service in the church.

Paul said cease from stealing, and then replace your stealing behavior with working. Paul said to start working – start making an honest living for yourself by your own efforts. The Greek word for "working" is ἐργάζομαι (*ergazomai*), which means "to labor, to work." Thus, Paul is admonishing you to work a real job, not a scheming job. You need the kind of job where you're receiving income regularly. Then Paul tells us why this is necessary. He said you need to start working so that you can share with those in need. "Share" in the Greek is μεταδίδωμι (*metadidómi*), which means "to share with someone, to those who need." So look at what Paul is saying. He's saying if we're going to have a community, you have to stop trying to take 'out' of the community and start putting 'into' the community. When they see large numbers of people, some people immediately begin to think, "What can I get out of this community?" You shouldn't want to steal from the church community. You should want to work so that you can share with those who are in need in the community.

If you are someone in the church community who is in need, this doesn't mean God is blessing others in the community just to give to you. If God desires to bless you through people in the church community, He will lay it on their hearts to bless you. You shouldn't go around the church asking people for money or to meet your needs. If you do this, you are a "church moocher" – someone who believes other people are supposed to take care of them because they don't have the means to take care of themselves. People outside of the church community do this all the time. Some people believe that the church is supposed to pay their bills and meet any need they have without even being a part of the church community. However, this is not what the Bible teaches.

4. Season your speech

> *Let no harmful language come from your mouth, only good words that are helpful in meeting the need, words that will benefit those who hear them. – Ephesians 4:29*

Paul said to let no harmful or corrupt word out of your mouth. The Greek word for "corrupt" is σαπρός (*sapros*), which means "to rot, putrid, base, filthy, without honor." This is a challenge for many people, especially those who get angry all the time. When Paul said, "Let no harmful language come from your mouth," the first thing many people think about is profanity. Now, profanity is organic in an anger environment, especially if you've been exposed to it. I don't know many saved, sanctified, filled with Holy Ghost, tongue-talking parents who have not said a cuss word to their child(ren) at least once! However, while it is not good to use profanity, this text goes beyond what we consider profanity. For example, what Jesus called the Pharisees would be regarded as profanity in our day and time. He called them whitewashed tombs full of dead men's bones (Matthew 23:27) – clean on the outside but filthy on the inside.

What Paul was saying here was that whatever comes out of your mouth should not be harmful to those who hear it, which means you ought to season your words with kindness. An example of this would be telling your child, "You're dumb and stupid! I wish I never had you. You're never going to become anything in life. You're just like your trifling daddy!" Or telling your spouse, "I hate you! I wish I never married you!" This is the kind of language that Paul is telling us to refrain from. If you're religious, you will be more upset at people who use profanity while you speak all kinds of harmful words to people in your life. You can't stand people who speak cuss words, but you verbally tear down your own kids and other people in your life. Just because harmful words are not profanity doesn't mean it's okay to speak them.

So what then are we to do? Paul said only speak words that are helpful or that build up and benefit those who hear them. There's an old cliché that says, "If you don't have anything nice to say, don't say anything at all." This is a good starting point, especially if it's difficult for you to say something nice. But Paul admonishes us to go a step further and speak life and not death in order to build community. Paul said to let your words be laced with grace. "Grace" in the Greek is χάρις (*charis*), meaning "favor." Thus, you must be intentional about what you say.

5. Be sensitive to the Holy Spirit

Don't cause grief to God's Ruach HaKodesh, for he has stamped you as his property until the day of final redemption. – Ephesians 4:30

You have to be sensitive to the Holy Spirit so that you won't grieve Him. The Greek word for "grieve" is λυπέω (*lupeó*), which means "to afflict with sorrow, sadden, to offend." When you tear people down, it's offensive to the Holy Spirit. Don't forget, the Holy Spirit is not a force; He's a Person. And when you tear down who He's trying to build up, you sadden and grieve Him. Thus, you don't want to grieve the Holy Spirit, because He is the One in whom you've been sealed to the day of redemption. Even Jesus said, "You can talk about Me but don't blaspheme the Holy Spirit" (Matthew 12:31-32). Blaspheming the Holy Spirit is an unpardonable sin, so you want to watch offending the Holy Spirit. The Greek word for "stamped" is σφραγίζω (*sphragízó*), which means "to seal, close up and make fast with a seal signet such as letters or books so that they may not be read."[1] Figuratively, it means "to se-

---

1 Zodhiates, S. (2000). *The complete word study dictionary: New Testament* (electronic ed.). Chattanooga, TN: AMG Publishers.

cure to someone, make sure, deliver over safely[2] by the Holy Spirit unto the day of redemption."

6. Strip off a bad attitude

> *Get rid of all bitterness, rage, anger, violent assertiveness and slander, along with all spitefulness. Instead, be kind to each other, tenderhearted; and forgive each other, just as in the Messiah God has also forgiven you. – Ephesians 4:31-32*

Then the last admonishment Paul gives is to strip off a bad attitude. What does that mean? Well, the first bad attitude Paul tells us to get rid of is bitterness. "Bitterness" in the Greek is πικρία (*pikria*), and it means "to strip off that irritated state of a man that keeps him or her always in animosity, makes him inclined to be harsh and to hold unfavorable opinions of others; makes him sour, crabby, and repulsive in general demeanor, that brings a scowl over the face and infuses the words of the tongue with venom." Then he said to get rid of rage (wrath), anger, and violent assertiveness. Wrath is a "more settled and deep flowing anger." Anger is "a temporary excitement and passion." Violent assertiveness is "outcries, shouting, and screaming." It is the cry of strife. Some people will cry aloud and scream out of anger, but they won't cry out and shout unto God in praise. Paul tells us to strip off an attitude that makes us negatively scream and shout at people, and then shout praises unto God.

The next characteristic of a bad attitude is slander. Slander is "evil speaking or speaking evil of someone," which results from enduring internal anger that manifests in revenge. When you let angry sit too long, you

2 Zodhiates, S. (2000). *The complete word study dictionary: New Testament* (electronic ed.). Chattanooga, TN: AMG Publishers.

end up speaking bad or negatively about people. The last characteristic he gives is spitefulness or malice. Malice is "bad heartedness, which is the root of all the attitudes and behavior." Thus, malice is the root of all the characteristics of a bad attitude.

Paul then said to replace a bad attitude by becoming something different. The Greek word for "be" is γίνομαι (*ginomai*), meaning "become." Paul tells us to become kind. "Kind" in the Greek is χρηστός (*chréstos*), which means "benevolent, good, useful." So we are to be benevolent and useful to one another. Then he said be tenderhearted – εὔσπλαγχνος (*eusplagchnos*), which means "inner organs referred to the seat of emotions; having the inner organ healthy or to have healthy bowels." So Paul is telling us to be good on the inside. Don't just be a front on the outside. Then he said to be forgiving – χαρίζομαι (*charizomai*), which means "to exercise grace." Why are we to do all of this? Because Christ has provided grace and forgiveness to us, who are unworthy; therefore, we should do the same. The Bible says that we should forgive 70 times seven in a day (Matthew 18:22). Why? Because God forgave us in Christ Jesus. There is nothing we can say to combat this expectation because not only did God forgive us in Christ Jesus, He continues to forgive us every day of our lives. Do you still need God's grace and forgiveness? Do you still need His mercy? Of course, you do!

Have you ever gone to God asking Him to forgive you for things you know you shouldn't have done, and God told you, "I'm not going to forgive you anymore. That's it. Your forgiveness limit is over"? No, because God has an endless capacity to forgive. And just like God forgives us, we should forgive others. So if there are people who do things to you and then ask you to forgive them, what are you to do? Forgive them. And what if they do it again? You forgive them again. Why does God tell us to keep forgiving like that? Because that's what He's doing for us now. It's not about who deserves to be forgiven and who doesn't. We can never have community as long as we keep holding offenses against each other. Therefore, we must give over to God and allow His Spirit to do a work of community within us.

When we read these exhortations and instructions from Paul, we hear him speaking to community life, not a life independent from the assembly. Instead, he admonishes the saints on how to conduct themselves in community and the outside world. The Bible cannot be read in terms of the individual but must be understood in the sense of physical gathering and the unity of community.

8 THE POWER OF UNITY

One of the things that I noticed about all of my academic degrees is that they all have a sense of unity or cooperation. My Ph.D. in Organizational Leadership centers around the unity and cooperation of organizations. My MBA focuses upon the strength of oneness and unity as the sparkplug for business design and production. When I was in the Global Executive MBA Program at Duke University's Fuqua School of Business, a course that I found most helpful was process management. This class focused on planning and controlling the complex processes used to produce goods and services provided by an organization, including production processes, process performance and improvement, inventory management, lean production, quality management, and the strategic role of operation in the firm. My Master of Economic Development and Entrepreneurship focused upon unifying efforts to bring economic development on the local, regional, state, and national levels for global competition. My behavioral science degrees focused on integrating and cooperating with yourself. It seems as if the goal of every good organization is unifying itself such that the organization can run smoothly and efficiently to bring about its intended purpose.

The image of God demonstrates the power of oneness, and we have discussed that power and how we must reflect that same image of God. In Genesis 1:26, God began by stating, "Let Us make man in Our image" – the *Elohim* (God in plurality – "Us"). We can read several unifying statements in scripture: Let Us go down (Genesis 11:7), Who shall I send, and who will go for Us (Isaiah 6:8). Though God is "Us," the presentation of God is oneness; God in three Persons but one God. What makes the triune Godhead so powerful and yet, so perplexing is the inability to separate the three Persons from the oneness of God. But the statement "Let Us make man in Our image" shows God's desire to make humanity like Himself – many but one. The statement to create man is a unity statement; God wants His people, though many, to be one or unified.

When God created man, he was created in the image of God. However, he was created both male and female, plurality within one structure. God then pulled the woman out of the man, and they once again become one. The concept of oneness is the concept that reflects the will, the way, and the Word of God. If we are to do anything on behalf of God, it must be according to the unity principle. Thus, in reflecting and representing God upon earth, the highest or greatest call of humanity reflects the oneness of God in unity. The highest call of the saved community is to operate in unity and agreement.

Since unity is the highest call of God for humanity, then disunity is the greatest attack against humanity. God uses unity or oneness, and Satan uses disunity and division. God operates in apostolic order; Satan operates in divide and conquer. God desires to gather us, and the enemy desires to divide us. God does His best work in community. And the devil does his best work in isolation. Unity or oneness is what God uses to produce efficiency and effectiveness; Satan uses disunity to produce chaos and confusion that ultimately ends in destruction and failure.

The Tower of Babel by Pieter Bruegel the Elder
(1563)

The story about the Tower of Babel (Genesis 11:1-9) teaches us the power of unity.

> *Now the whole world had one language and a common speech. As people moved eastward, they found a plain in Shinar and settled there. They said to each other, "Come, let's make bricks and bake them thoroughly." They used brick instead of stone, and tar for mortar. Then they said, "Come, let us build ourselves a city, with a tower that reaches to the heavens, so that we may make a name for ourselves; otherwise we will be scattered over the face of the whole earth." But the LORD came down to see the city and the tower the people were building. The LORD said, "If as one people speaking the same*

language they have begun to do this, then nothing they plan to do will be impossible for them. Come, let us go down and confuse their language so they will not understand each other." So the LORD scattered them from there over all the earth, and they stopped building the city. That is why it was called Babel—because there the LORD confused the language of the whole world. From there the LORD scattered them over the face of the whole earth.

The people, who spoke one common language, came together in Shinar.

- They created a **plan** – "Come, let's make bricks and bake them thoroughly."

- They had a **purpose** – "Come, let us build ourselves a city, with a tower that reaches to the heavens, so that we may make a name for ourselves; otherwise we will be scattered over the face of the whole earth."

  - Something within them caused them to desire to remain together and not be disbursed around the globe.

- They had a **process** of execution – Their desire to build focused upon self-preservation.

The Bible states that Adonai came down to see the tower the people were building and saw that the people were united. Then God said, "If as one people speaking the same language they have begun to do this, then nothing they plan to do will be impossible for them" (v. 6). Then God in plurality decided to go down (an anthropomorphic expression – meaning it didn't escape His attention) and confuse their speech so they could not understand each other. The Prophet Amos wrote about the general principle of agreement through interaction, stating how can two walk together except they agree on the details of the walk (Amos 3:3). Thus, they stopped building, and it is called "Babel" for this reason, which means "confusion." It's important to note that God disrupted the unity of the people in Shinar because they were unified against Him. The people said, "Come, let's build ourselves a city with a tower that has its top reaching up into heaven, so that we can make a name for ourselves and not be scattered all over the earth" (Genesis 11:4). Though God is a God of unity, He doesn't support unified efforts against His will or His purpose.

Unity is the biblical way; thus, when we walk with God, He desires that we walk in unity. The church is called to walk in oneness or unity of vision and purpose. There can be no unity of purpose within the local church unless we physically gather. The Bible constantly repeats, in both testaments, that the people of God are defined as a people, not a person. And in order to represent God on earth, we must do the same as physically gathered people, not individuals. Thus, if an individual uses their free will to not persevere in God, they do not disrupt the integrity of the church. They just disrupt their integrity as an individual. One person's spiritual shortcomings did not disrupt the corporate integrity of Israel.

The church is called to unity; thus, when Paul wrote to the church at Philippi, he addressed the issue of disunity and disruption by outsiders who were attempting to disassemble the corporate gathering and created individual silos of subjectivity and rebellion against spiritual authority. Thus, Paul wrote, "fulfill my joy by being like-minded, having the same love, being of one accord, of one mind" (Philippians 2:2). Paul was calling for the unity of community in physical gathering, not through social distancing, but through physical bonding in physical gathering. The church must gather to be the church. However, when the church gathers, we must never forget that both the visible and invisible churches are present in that gathering.

When the church physically gathers, there are sure to be people in the gathering who are disruptive, repulsive, and rebellious, which the Bible refers to as "tare" (Matthew 13:24-30). Yet, the church must continue to function even with the distractions from those who say they are "modern-day Israel" and are not. Many pretenders in the church are not there for the vision and purpose of the Kingdom of God. They have their own agenda; they have needs of physical fellowship and belonging that are not spiritually nor Christ-motivated. Some people come to church for dating and marital purposes, community outreach, altruistic endeavors, and the like, but are not there to seek the Kingdom of God and His righteousness through spiritual submission to spiritual authority and the Word of God. As long as the visible church exists, the church as a whole will be impacted by those who are insincere about their gathering – concerned about the cares of this world, the desires for other things, and the deceitfulness of riches (Mark 4:19).

Nehemiah, in Babylonian exile, had a high assignment to be the Persian king's cupbearer. However, he was grieved about the separation and the condition of Israel upon their return to Jerusalem and attempt to regather in physical gathering and worship. Nehemiah was briefed about the condition of Israel and set out, by the permission of the king, to rebuild the walls of Jerusalem and restore the Temple, Israel's physical gathering. In order for Israel to be fortified, they understood that there must be a 'coming together;' thus, Nehemiah began his campaign to restore the walls of Jerusalem (Nehemiah 2:1-20).

His first order of business was to get a group that he could physically gather with and assist him in calling the tribes and people to physically gather. They were challenged with great resistance from those on both the outside and inside; those who had their own individual agendas and those who were compromised in their commitment to Torah. However, through Nehemiah's leadership, they overcame astronomical antagonism and opposition and rebuilt the walls by physically coming together. Thus, the book of Nehemiah attributes the success of the project to the people coming together and working in unity. The book records that "the people had a mind to work" (Nehemiah 4:6).

It is obvious why Paul, who had a Jewish background, would work so tirelessly to ensure corporate unity in physical gathering, writing, "endeavoring to keep the unity of the Spirit in the bond of peace" (Ephesians 4:3). He consistently insisted and instructed the people of God to remain unified to accomplish the mission of the church in a secular world that had little to no tolerance for their mission. The mission of the church is to transform lives that are connected to this world and challenge them to depart from their secular and sinful passions and come into the Kingdom of our Lord, Jesus the Messiah.

The psalter King David wrote this about the power of physical gathering and unity:

> *"Oh, how good, how pleasant it is for brothers to live together in harmony. It is like fragrant oil on the head that runs down over the beard, over the beard of Aharon, and flows down on the collar of his robes. It is like the dew of Hermon that settles on the mountains of Tziyon. For it was there that Adonai ordained the blessing of everlasting life." – Psalm 133:1-3*

David was a proponent of a unified kingdom that physically gathered to represent God's Kingdom upon the earth and among the nations. Dwelling in unity brings about peace and special anointing, released through apostolic order and commanded blessings. The blessings are commanded where the gathering is held!

Solomon, the son of David, wrote:

> *There is one alone, without companion: He has neither son nor brother. Yet there is no*

end to all his labors, Nor is his eye satisfied with riches. But he never asks, "For whom do I toil and deprive myself of good?" This also is vanity and a grave misfortune. Two are better than one, Because they have a good reward for their labor. For if they fall, one will lift up his companion. But woe to him who is alone when he falls, For he has no one to help him up. Again, if two lie down together, they will keep warm; But how can one be warm alone? Though one may be overpowered by another, two can withstand him. And a threefold cord is not quickly broken. – Ecclesiastes 4:8-14

Solomon, in this text, is addressing the futility of isolation and how unproductive one person is working alone. Even God stated that it's not good for man to be alone; we need some form of companionship beyond romantic relationship, the type of union that brings about support in accomplishing the task that God has placed before us. It is not God's revealed pattern for us to have to pull ourselves up by our own bootstraps in isolation. "Pull yourself up by your own bootstraps" is an American idiom: to improve your situation by your own efforts; to succeed only by one's own efforts or abilities.

James Joyce alluded to it in *Ulysses*, 1922: "There were others who had forced their way to the top from the lowest rung by the aid of their bootstraps." Our faith is not to be lived in a vacuum nor achieved through individualistic efforts.

Two are better than one. The Midrash (or Jewish commentary) states, "Two are better when they study Torah together than one who labors alone, for if they fall, the one will lift up his brother." The *Talmud* says, "A man without a companion is like a left hand without the right. Consider how much having only one hand hinders productivity. When both hands are available, much more can be accomplished, and every activity is easier. How much greater is the production of two people doing a task than if the labor is restricted to only one?" Thus, unity lends itself to productivity.

God calls the church to assembly based upon this simple principle: united we stand and divided we fall (Mark 3:24). The church is dependent upon all of the members of the body to operate cohesively to bring the heavenly vision to pass. You must not ever view your work for God as something that is simply between you and God. God doesn't cut private contracts; He is a corporate God, and we all work in tandem with one another to accomplish a complex task. Physical gathering for the people of God is mandatory. Without it, there is no people of God, just an individual who is subjectively representing themselves in the name of God. You must be connected to the body and doing your part, nourishing and nurturing the body through your impartation to the whole, not working simply on yourself.

Consider the Lord's Prayer, the actual prayer that Jesus prayed for His disciples found in John 17:20-21, "I do not pray for these alone, but also for those who will believe in Me through their word; that they all may be one, as You, Father, are in Me, and I in You; that they also may be one in Us, that the world may believe that You sent Me." Jesus' prayer was that believers would be one in God – from His disciples to future disciples. The church cannot be one without the words of those who are sent by God to preach and teach His Word and represent Him in the world (Romans 10:14-15). The church is called to represent oneness in the world, nationally, and in local communities, and we do so only when we physically gather.

Because unity through community is the plan and way of God, Satan will make every attempt to destroy the unity of Israel and the church. Remember, he is the one that created disunity between Adam and Eve and disunity between the human race and God. Satan entices people to make asinine attempts to move forward without God, utilizing their own intellect and rationality. A walk with God is a walk of faith, and as long as people lean on their own understanding, God cannot direct their paths (Proverbs 3:5-6). There is a way that seems right to man, but the end is destruction

(Proverbs 14:12). When we attempt to move outside of the pack, we set ourselves up for individual destruction and corporate embarrassment outside of the herd.

Think about one of the challenges that countries face today concerning COVID-19 – attaining herd immunity through vaccinations. It has not been an easy road to get enough of the population vaccinated so we can live a relatively safe life from COVID-19. The challenge is getting everyone to participate for the whole to be more protected. However, some refuse to participate, therefore, putting the whole in jeopardy. Likewise, oneness is vital in the church. God is not trying to simply move the individual; He is leading the herd through His appointed shepherds (Jeremiah 3:15, Ephesians 4:11). There is no place for a goat mentality, because it places the pack in danger.

Maverick Christianity has always been a threat to the perpetuity and effectiveness of the church. The church cannot be defined through the acts of the individual but through the actions of the whole, even against and above the acts of the individual. Thus, the individual, who is a part of the invisible church, must walk in cadence with the corporate body. The invisible church cannot function in disagreement; it must walk in agreement based upon order and protocol.

Another factor that weakens unity in the body is the bitter seeds of self-centeredness. Self-centeredness is the attitude of "me first;" it is the belief that the perverted trinity – me, myself, and I – comes before anything in life. When the spirit of self-centeredness is allowed to freely operate, unity is impossible and corporate mobility is stagnated. Self-centered people will always have problems with church leadership and authority because no one can tell them what to do. They will have a problem with ministry participation because their time, family, career, etc., comes first. They will also have challenges in tithing and giving because they utilize 100% of their funds to fund their lifestyle without considering prioritizing the Kingdom.

Another critical factor that destroys unity is the lack of communication and/or communication issues. One of the top reasons for marital failure, business failure, parental failure, and ministry failure is communication. The church has to be a place where we speak the truth in love, regardless of the possible effects on the individual. The number one vehicle of communication in the church is the pulpit, where all the members must gather to hear the corporate Word of God. Then the next vehicle of communication in the church is corporate prayer, where we talk to God as a community.

Areas of communication include the following:

- The process of equipping the saints for the work of ministry involves discussing your spiritual gifts that empower the Body of Christ.

- Corporate communication is sent electronically or physically to promptly make the church aware of events, meetings, and activities.
- Communication for accountability, such as when the members communicate their attendance so that the church can be aware of the membership's well-being.
- Conflict resolution – where it is appropriate for members to share personal conflicts with the person that they are offended with and be committed to the process of resolution. When conflict is not resolved through the proper biblical way of resolution, it will lead to a drift and a divide in the membership.

The last area I would like to point out that attacks the unity in the body is offense or disobedience to the Word of God. Through the principle of divide and conquer, Satan masters individuals and uses their weaknesses to destroy the church, which he hates. However, he cannot contend with the true church, the invisible church, the blood-bought believers, who are born again and have prioritized the Kingdom.

We must become one in God's purpose to accomplish God's will. We must embrace these principles of unity if we are going to walk in the unity of community in physical gatherings. In my over 36 years of executive ministry, I have seen so many people taken out of the body through Satan's strategies, as mentioned earlier. The majority of those I have seen taken out never make it back to the fold because they become distant through separation from the fire of church gathering.

To maintain the fire in your walk with God, you must walk with people and be around people that support your biblical values and principles for living. The Midrash states, "If one forgets his laws, the other can re-store it to him." When you are around people with a secular mentality and agenda, the Bible says bad company corrupts good morals. A little leaven, a typology of sin, leavens the whole loaf (1 Corinthians 5:6; 15:33).

To maintain a conscious effort towards the things of God, you must be one with your corporate community. This involves:

1. Seeing the same thing (vision)

2. Speaking the same thing (communication)

    a. "Come, let us make bricks and bake them thoroughly...come, let us make ourselves a city and a tower that reaches the heavens." This principle got God's attention to act against Babel.

3. Follow sent leadership – imitate your leader (1 Corinthians 1:1-2)

4. Don't allow anyone to bring division between you and your church family

    a. Paul wrote, "Now I plead with you, brethren, by the name of our Lord Jesus Christ, that you all speak the same thing, and that there be no divisions among you, but that you be per-fectly joined together in the same mind and in the same judgment" (1 Corinthians 1:10-11). The goal of the body is to be united in vision and physically gathered to receive the in-structions of the Lord and participate in com-munity life in worship.

5. Walk in agreement with one another, "For where two or three are gathered together in My name, I am there in the midst of them" (Matthew 18:20).

6. Walk in agreement with the Word of God, "And with this the words of the prophets agree, just as it is written" (Acts 15:15).

Thus, we pray – make us one, even as Jesus and the Father are one!

9

THE PROTECTION OF FELLOWSHIP

The unity of community is the design of God, and the scriptures declare that the early church was a church that thrived through the unity of community. Acts 2 speaks of how the church subscribed to the apostolic teachings of the apostles and submitted to their leadership in mind, heart, and soul (Acts 4:32). In my analysis of the scripture and the Newer Testament church, the two most important gifts God has bestowed upon you and me are covering and community.

The devil loves working and deceiving in isolation; we have biblical examples of what happened to Eve, Judas, Demas, and Samson. The reason Satan prefers isolation is that he operates from the premise of deception, confusion, and ignorance. These three areas are the three areas that Paul warned believers to be aware of in his epistles. The devil is a deceiver and he is good at what he does. The Bible states that he appears as an angel of light (2 Corinthians 11:14). The devil is the author of confusion and stirs it up, but God is the author of peace (1 Corinthians 14:33). The devil wants to keep you uninformed or ignorant (1 Corinthians 12:3, Romans 12:3, 1 Peter 2:15, 2 Timothy 2:23). Ignorance and foolish travel to gather as a team, and Satan uses them as an invisible trap to remove you from your walk with God unknowingly.

God has given Kingdom citizens both a covering through apostolic leadership and a community (the church) to live out their faith. It is obvious that in the 1st century, they enjoyed and took full advantage of these two gifts. They gave heed to the apostles' doctrine, and they fellowshipped from house to house daily (Acts 2:42, 46). The power of fellowship is what assists in keeping you grounded in God. Walking with Jesus was never intended to be a lonely journey but a corporate walk with a community mission.

Satan desires to sift you like wheat, but the Bible states that the weapon used against the strong believer is the weapon of unequally yoked fellowship. Thus, Christ warns us that over time, the un-fellowshipped believer stops participating in the things of God's Kingdom due to their newfound interest and relationships with the unsaved and/or religious but not relational believer. Christ states that they fall among thorns, which choked the Word out of their life (Mark 4:19). This is a fellowship issue! Remember, fellowship is the coming together of like-minded individuals who have mutual interests and a collective goal; this is the ekklesia of God.

The Parable of the Sower or the Parable of Pre-imminence (as I have named it), lets us know what kind of environment can put once-strong believers in an environment of deception, confusion, and ignorance: the cares of this world, the deceitfulness of riches, and the desire for other things. Satan deceives us through misaligned relationships with people who do not have a Kingdom agenda. Perhaps they go to church (deception, angel of light), perhaps you don't understand why you are having such a hard time (confusion – 1 Peter 2:21), or perhaps they talk spiritual talk (foolish and ignorant – 1 Peter 2:15, 2 Timothy 2:23). This is a fellowship issue! Your associations and affiliations influence your thoughts and philosophical positions. If you find pleasure and enjoyment in carnal fellowship, you eventually will be drawn into their thought processes. When you compromise your position, it's because your convictions and values were not strong enough to draw them into your world. But their position was strong enough to draw you to theirs. This is a widespread occurrence when people fail to participate in corporate spiritual gatherings; instead, they turn to carnal or compromised gatherings.

Satan is determined to cause you to disavow God's truth and walk in a different understanding than what you were taught about Christ and the Word. He comes to kill, steal, and destroy your walk and relationship with Christ (John 10:10). Jesus teaches us that the enemy desires to devour you by causing you to regurgitate the Word of God. He is attempting to choke you to spiritual death. This 'choking the Word out' is one of the themes of the book of Hebrews. The believer who begins to drift from the Word (Hebrews 2:1-4) will doubt the Word (Hebrews 3:7-4:13) and soon will become dull towards the Word (Hebrews 5:12-6:20), which ultimately leads to despising the Word. Willfully sinning is the result of despising the Word! The author of the book of Hebrews, who I attribute to Paul but ultimately the Holy Spirit, suggests that the one-time believer can abandon their convictions about Christ, therefore, causing them to forfeit their claims to eternal life with God. The text states that instead of the benefits of heaven, this person will now experience the torment of hell, because they got caught up in inappropriate relationships. They are now facing judgment and fiery indignation, which will devour all the adversaries of God.

Hebrews 10 brings to light the power of community and fellowship, stating that the abrogation of the Law of Moses was confirmed by two to three witnesses. Then death without mercy was applied (Hebrews 10:28-29). Thus, the text suggests that if death upon the witness of two to three witnesses was ascribed to the violator of the Law of Moses, what do you think happens to the one who has trampled the Son of God underfoot, counted the blood of the covenant by which He was sanctified a common thing, and insulted the Spirit of grace? The implication of the scripture is that God will judge the believer for not guarding their faith in Christ through their covering and their community.

He then calls the believer to the following saying, "But recall the former days in which, after you were illuminated, you endured a great struggle with sufferings" (Hebrews 10:32). The writer calls the believer to remember how when you first got saved, you were made a spectacle both by reproaches and tribulations. He said recount when you became companions of those who were so treated (Hebrews 10:33). The Greek word for "companions" is κοινωνός (koinōnos), which means "as one who fellowships and shares something in common with another partner; partaker, fellow participant, companion." The inference of the writing is that believers experienced their life in the Kingdom together in fellowship. It was the physical gathering that encouraged the saints to persevere and handle the hardships of persecution and tribulation. He further wrote to the church to recollect when you had a heart of compassion for your covering and joyfully accepted the plundering of your goods, knowing that you have a better and enduring possession for yourselves in heaven (Hebrews 10:34). The church was compassionate and considerate of the challenges of the person who served as a spiritual covering for the church.

Lastly, he admonished them not to cast away their confidence or boldness, which has a great reward or payment of wages (Hebrews 10:35). The Greek word for "cast away" is ἀποβάλλω (apoballō), which means "throw off, cast away." The church is called to be bold or have confidence in their witness of the Lord Jesus

Christ, which is reinforced through the fellowship of the saints. The challenge of the 21st century church is focus – making the main thing the main thing. It is not the entertainment of a worship center that draws us together. We gather to hear the instructional Word of the Lord for the mission and how we are to behave while in the world but not become of the world (1 John 2:15-17). It is the interaction of the saints that provides us with a foundation for boldness in a society that is contradistinctive from the culture of the Kingdom.

God has given the believer a great safety net through the formation of community – the wisdom of a covering who feeds the sheep with knowledge and understanding (Jeremiah 3:15). The author of the epistle to the Hebrew followers of Jesus, who were being persecuted for their faith in Jesus the Messiah, repetitively reminded them of the power of a covering and community. The ministry of the shepherd is to have rule or reflective authority over you for you to clearly understand the will and the Word of the Lord for your life. The spiritual covering is released by God to shepherd the flock to watch for their souls, as those who must give an account for the lives of the sheep (Hebrews 13:17). The Bible instructs the followers of Jesus to obey and submit to spiritual authority, who has been ordained by God, to ensure that the followers of Jesus do not fall prey to the trap of the enemy, who is deceptive and exceedingly cunning.

The writer also suggests that frustrating spiritual authority is to frustrate God. If you frustrate your leader, that is God's way of communicating His displeasure with the behavior of God's people (Hebrews 13:17). The writer states that your covering is to be a model of how to walk with God saying, "Remember those who rule over you, who have spoken the word of God to you, whose faith follow, considering the outcome of their conduct (Hebrews 13:7). Jesus Christ is the same yesterday, today, and forever (Hebrews 13:8).

The spiritual covering is a spiritual blessing sent from God. Though they are not God, they represent God on earth and assist the believers in becoming who and what God has designed them to be. Without your spiritual covering, you cannot have an official assembly of the saints. Spiritual leadership is the official representatives of the Kingdom and the leaders of the community. The role of the spiritual covering is the foundation of the spiritual community or the church of the Lord Jesus Christ. Your covering is your gift from God (Jeremiah 3:15, Ephesians 4:11). Spiritual authority should take care of the flock of God; they are the thermostats of the community. Peter wrote the following:

> *Therefore, I urge the congregation leaders among you, as a fellow-leader and witness to the Messiah's sufferings, as well as a sharer in the glory to be revealed: shepherd the flock of God that is in your care, exercising oversight not out of constraint, but willingly, as God wants; and not out of a desire for dishonest gain, but with enthusiasm; also not as machers domineering over those in your care, but as people who become examples to the flock. Then, when the Chief Shepherd appears, you will receive glory as your unfading crown. – 1 Peter 5:1-4*

The spiritual leadership of the church serves as both a covering and example for Kingdom living. Thus, the body of believers under their leadership is commanded to follow their lead.

All of this language clearly speaks to the church in physical gatherings. It is impossible to interpret these passages in the context of social distancing or the internet church. The church must gather physically to be the church in the world. The covering and the community are essential in defining the church, and both keep the believer safe and confident in the Kingdom as they walk out a counterculture life. The separation from that which is secular empowers the believer to walk among the secular as the holy people of God. People separated from a covering and the church community have been duped by Satan; he has taken advantage of them. They have an inability to recognize Satan's works because of the lack of a watchman, who watches over their souls. If we could protect ourselves, God would not have required nor sent a watchman with special spiritual skills and tools to recognize the enemy beyond what a layperson can recognize. Physical gathering is where you encounter your covering and your community and experience the commanded blessings based upon the unity factor.

Why Fellowship?

Finally, with regard to physical gathering and fellowship, the writer of Hebrews provides us with the "why" of fellowship:

> So, brothers, we have confidence to use the
> way into the Holiest Place opened by the

blood of Yeshua. He inaugurated it for us as a new and living way through the parokhet, by means of his flesh. We also have a great cohen over God's household. Therefore, let us approach the Holiest Place with a sincere heart, in the full assurance that comes from trusting — with our hearts sprinkled clean from a bad conscience and our bodies washed with pure water. Let us continue holding fast to the hope we acknowledge, without wavering; for the One who made the promise is trustworthy. And let us keep paying attention to one another, in order to spur each other on to love and good deeds, not neglecting our own congregational meetings, as some have made a practice of doing, but, rather, encouraging each other." – *Hebrews 10:19-25*

One of the most dangerous things a believer can do is try to live for Christ in isolation. The Kingdom is a public, not a private, call; it is a life of community, not individuality. You and I have been called into a communal faith that is based on individual or personal decisions but corporate involvement. The devil loves to isolate believers because there he can deceive them, appealing to their natural or fleshly conclusions based upon their personal convenience. The enemy knows that you and I are prone to make wrong decisions under duress, decisions that benefit our comfort and not necessarily the Kingdom of God. The Bible states that there is a way that seems right to man, but the end thereof is destruction (Proverbs 14:12)! The Bible states that many are the plans in a man's heart, but the Lord's purpose shall prevail (Proverbs 19:21). How does this happen, beloved, when the plans of our hearts are seemingly so pure and the logic seems so credible? It is because when you and I are in certain seasons of our lives that we don't desire to be in, we can rationalize ourselves into more comfortable choices.

This is the rationale behind "safety in the multitude of counsel" (Proverbs 11:14). You do not have the ability alone to discern the different attacks of the enemy. We have to remember what happened to Eve, Saul, the great kings, the prophets, and don't forget Judas, Demas, and the church. The devil would like you to interpret your life in a vacuum. However, God has given you two essential gifts that can assist you in making spiritual decisions and choices that will help you remain in the will of God – a covering and community. Remember, the enemy wants to get you out of the will of God through giving up or giving out, but the Bible tells us we will receive God's rewards if we do not faint (Galatians 6:9). When you become a part of the Kingdom of God, God places you under His delegated authority and within His Kingdom community (Acts 2:47).

We all know the great importance of spiritual leadership and embrace it, even though it is a challenge for some. Even though we embrace the concept of spiritual leadership through a preacher, many of us tend to diminish the importance of Kingdom fellowship. What is fellowship and why is it important? Fellowship is "the coming to gather of like-minded individuals who have mutual interest and a collective goal." Hence, the Bible warns us about being unequally yoked with unbelievers, stating there is no fellowship between daylight and darkness. Fellowship cannot exist when mutual interest and mutual goals do not exist (2 Corinthians 6:14). The enemy puts us in environments and around people, who are not like-minded, so we can be influenced by darkness without our awareness. But God instructs us to fellowship with other believers to influence us towards the will of God and Kingdom purpose.

The strength of the early church was their daily fellowship; they met house to house. They were branded as having weird gatherings, like *agape* love feasts, because of the strength and frequencies of their fellowship. You may be saying to yourself, "I hang around believers when I go to church – isn't that enough?" But the Bible states that the early church met daily from house to house (Acts 2:46). Remember, a threefold cord is not easily broken (Ecclesiastes 4:12)! Some of us are now saying post-COVID – "Isn't Zoom enough - isn't that fellowship?" I will address this question in a later chapter but until then, let me answer this question rabbinic style (with a question). Is a Zoom call enough to maintain a marriage? While you may become familiar with someone online, you must spend physical time to have a healthy relationship.

You have to watch the enemy because the presence of grace can be used as a tool the enemy uses to deceive you into thinking that your choices and affiliations don't matter because you are 'saved by grace.' The above-mentioned text (Hebrews 10) reiterates several things that assist the believer in understanding who they are in Christ, how they are in Christ, and what they are to do as the household of faith. The scripture declares that we are saved and sanctified by the blood of Christ and that Christ's blood was effective for our sin forever (Hebrews 10:12)! We don't have to live to be forgiven — we are forgiven. Thank God that we are forgiven today by the blood of the great High Priest, Christ. He sacrificed His life for us and is now sitting at the right hand of the Father, waiting until His enemies are made His footstool. By His offering, He has perfected those who are being set apart forever (Hebrews 10:14). Through the blood of the Lamb, we can go to God with boldness and confidence that He hears us through the blood of Christ. He made a way for us (Hebrews 10:19)! We have a High Priest over the house of God who intercedes for us (Hebrews 10:21)!

Exhortations from Hebrews 10

Let us draw near to God with a sincere heart, not with guilt, having our hearts sprinkled from an evil conscience and our bodies washed with pure water. Only a priest can draw near to God in this manner – the ministry of intercession (v. 22)!

Let us hold fast the confession of our faith without wavering, for He is faithful who promised. Don't go back to Judaism (legalism) (v. 23)!

> Let us consider one another in order to stir up love and good works. Let us not neglect the fellowship but exhort one another as we see the evil days of deception approaching! The emphasis is not simply what you get out of fellowship but also what you contribute to fellowship. We are to stir up love and exhort, promoting good works (vv. 24-25).

The inference here is that we are not to opt-out of physical fellowship. The scripture clearly states do not forsake the assembly of the saints. "Forsake" is the Greek term ἐγκαταλείπω (egkataleipó), which means "to leave in the lurch, to forsake." This verb is a present tense which suggests to never forsake the assembly. The term "assembly" here is ἐπισυναγωγή (episunagógé), which means "a gathering together, assembly." In the compound, it indicates the common responsibility. The term should be understood as simply the regular gathering together of Christian believers for worship and exhortation in a particular place.

The term suggests that it is the responsibility of the believer to gather together as a manner of life in the Kingdom. The text states that so-called believers will demean and diminish the importance of physical gathering at some point, and it will become an everyday habit. The Greek word for "habit" is ἔθος (ethos), meaning "custom, habit." But as the habit of no longer feeling that physical gathering is meaningful increases, the true believer is to encourage or entreat others to physically gather. The Greek word for "entreat" is παρακαλέω (parakaleō), which means "to encourage, to entreat, which is the same term used in Romans 12:1." The term is used for the call of soldiers to order and attention; it is the rallying and gathering of the troops for service. Physical gathering is an assembling of the saints to help us handle the times that are in opposition to the message of Christ. Still, we must remain conscious and encouraged by physically gathering and encouraging one another for the task.

10 THE PRIORITY OF FELLOWSHIP

We have been discussing the significance of fellowship and how vital physical gatherings are as it pertains to having a relationship with Christ and His church. The act of physically gathering is a special gift dedicated to the people of God that provides a level of protection through a special covering and the community of the saints. The church of Jesus Christ is always in physical gathering and fellowship, adding to and contributing to the growth of the body. Fellowship is not simply an optional act or routine that the church does; it is the priority of our relationship with God. Consider what John the beloved disciple wrote concerning the issue of fellowship, "But if we are walking in the light, as he is in the light, then we have fellowship with each other, and the blood of his Son Yeshua purifies us from all sin. If we claim not to have sinned, we are deceiving ourselves, and the truth is not in us. If we acknowledge our sins, then, since he is trustworthy and just, he will forgive them and purify us from all wrongdoing" (1 John 1:7-9).

Fellowship was one of the key practices of the early church. In fact, Pentecost cites fellowship as one of the priorities of the early church. Fellowship, as mentioned in earlier chapters, is from the Greek word κοινωνία (*koinonia*), which refers to a relationship characterized by sharing in common fellowship, participation (1 John 1:3). The term "fellowship" is the opposite of the word κακία (*kakia*), which means "dislike or hatefulness." So fellowship implies a sense of liking those with whom you fellowship. John wrote about two levels of fellowship: the first is with God and the second is with each other. The believer is to have both a vertical and horizontal relationship with God and God's people.

When we examine the Newer Testament church, the scriptures declare that they first gave heed to the apostles' doctrine and then to fellowship (Acts 2:42). We have defined fellowship as "the medium of exchange that takes place between people who have a common goal and mutual interests." Thus, the Bible states there is no fellowship between daylight and darkness, between righteousness and lawlessness, between believers and unbelievers, between Christ and Belial, and between the temple of God with idols (2

Corinthians 6:14-18). Fellowship was so vital to spiritual longevity that it was the first spiritual practice of the early church. Fellowship provided a protective environment that would assist in shielding believers and their faith from those who desired to diminish and destroy it through the influence of Satan. In fact, fellowship was so vital to spiritual perseverance that the writer of Hebrews suggests that it is the practice that encourages and exhorts believers in times of spiritual indifference and apostasy. God designed it to stop the enemy from isolating the saints and imparting deceptive ideologies and ungodly appetites. Without physical gathering and fellowship, the believer will become highly vulnerable and subject to the philosophies of Satan.

The enemy loves to isolate the believer, especially during seasons of duress and transitions. This is why the Bible states that there is safety in the multitude of counsel, however, not just any counsel (Proverbs 11:14). The Bible also states that bad company corrupts good morals, and blessed is the man who walks not in the counsel of the ungodly nor takes the sinner's position (1 Corinthians 15:33, Psalm 1:1). Remember that Satan uses close relationships that are prone to carnality to influence us from the ultimate will of God. Fellowship can be used either for good or evil. Thus, we see him using Eve with Adam, Delilah with Samson, Jezebel with Ahab, Herodias and Herod, and Peter with Jesus. Christ warns that the greatest challenge will be those in your household (Micah 7:6, Matthew 10:36). The Parable of Preeminence also provides insight concerning Satan's desire to cause us to fall into improper relationships that are not aligned with a Kingdom agenda; at some point, they choke the Word out of you. Therefore, the scriptures admonish believers to not forsake the assembling of themselves together as the manner of some (Hebrews 10:25).

As mentioned earlier, two of the most powerful gifts God gives you, outside of salvation and the Holy Spirit, are His gifts of covering and fellowship through community. This is why the early church met from house to house daily. This also serves as the reasoning for small groups, which is a practice utilized globally today with significant discipleship implications. Fellowship becomes the environment in which faith, hope, and love can be fostered and guarded. Fellowship is the prescription of God designed to assist believers in maintaining their relationship and walk God.

While fellowship with believers is the main key to protecting your relationship with God, fellowship with God is the key to preserving your relationship with both God and man. The Bible states that the first thing that God established with man was relationship or 'relate-ability.' We were created in the likeness of God or with the ability to have fellowship. Adam and Eve's relationship was built upon a common goal and mutual interest – to tend and keep (abad and shamar) the Garden of Eden. The garden was the place of mutuality; it was the place or atmosphere of God and man. The infraction of humanity upon God's commandment caused broken fellowship. Man's interest became misaligned. He no longer desired to fellowship with God; he desired to be like God and develop his own goals and interests (Genesis 3:5). Thus, the fall of man is about disfellowship or broken relationship.

Salvation, however, is about restoration and reconciliation of relationship. Relationship is the substratum of fellowship. You cannot have fellowship without relationship. The root of the word "relationship" is "relate," which suggests things in common or mutual interests. Thus, God restored His relationship with man and created a platform for fellowship. The relationship was based upon faith, forgiveness, focus, and friendship. We are saved by faith in the finished work of Christ upon the cross and have been guaranteed the forgiveness of sins – past, present, and future. We have a mutual focus upon the Kingdom of God and have been made friends, not enemies of God.

Friendship suggests mutual trust and favor; remember, the Bible states that friends are made for adversity (Proverbs 17:17). We have a relationship with God through the blood of the Lamb, and we have fellowship with God through the light of His Word. David stated that His word is a lamp unto my feet and a light unto my pathway (Psalm 119:105). It is the Word of God that provides the basis for fellowship with God. The light of God's Word reveals His interests and His goals; thus, to remain in fellowship with God, there are two primary drivers: the blood and the Word. The church is the blood-bought community of God that gathers around the Word of God (1 Corinthians 6:20). During the reformational era of John Calvin, he was asked how he was so successful in spreading his message of reformation to so many people. Calvin simply responded, "I just raised the banner of the word, and the real saints rallied around it."

In 1 John 1:3, 7, the Apostle John spoke of the necessity of fellowship with God based upon a relationship with God. John declared that we have had the privilege of experiencing the Word of life that imparts eternal life. Through Him, others may be partakers of fellowship with them. But then John stated that our fellowship is indeed with the Father and with His Son Jesus Christ. Thus, John encouraged fellowship with the apostles and with God. He suggested that fellowship with the apostles was the means to fellowship with God. When we physically gather, we do not do so to simply gather with like-minded people, but with people who have been transformed by the renewing of their minds through the teachings of the apostles or fivefold ministry gifts. We gather to hear the preacher, not simply to see our friends; The preacher's presence transforms the environment from a social environment to a spiritual environment. The sheep gather to be fed by the shepherd – "as the deer pants towards the water..." (Psalm 42:1). The sheep cannot wait to get to church so that they can bask in the pillar of the truth, because it is the apostles' doctrine that provides the believer with the message of salvation – past, present, and future.

John's message is that God is light, and in Him, there is no darkness at all. The Greek word for darkness is σκότος (skotos). Let's get a better understanding of darkness. It is 1) literally, an enveloping sphere where light (φῶς:- phos) is absent (darkness, gloom, obscurity); in relation to the world, as the primitive chaos before light was created (2 Corinthians 4:6); idiomatically, literally the outer darkness, i.e., the place of punishment, as the region of future exclusion from the Kingdom of God (Matthew 8:12); (2) figuratively, as an absence of moral and spiritual renewal or ignorance, lack of understanding (Acts 26.18); metaphorically, as the domain under the authority of the devil and demons' realm of evil, the evil world (Luke 22:53, Ephesians 6.12).[1] Thus, if we say that we have fellowship with Him and walk in darkness, we lie (ψεύδομαι: *psuedomai*, tell what is not true, mislead) and do not practice the truth. Hence, John suggests that walking in darkness is not walking in a relationship with God.

Darkness here implies a state, not a situation. Darkness refers to being ignorant and estranged from God through the blindness of spiritual sight. Thus, John wrote in his gospel and epistle about the contrast between darkness and light, suggesting that darkness is the state of those who do not have a relationship with Christ. Yet, when they come to know Him, they are enlightened by Him. The relationship with Christ is a light relationship that breaks the power of darkness (2 Corinthians 6:16). Paul wrote that He has rescued us from the power of darkness and transferred us to the Kingdom of His Son (Colossians 1:13). He also wrote, in Ephesians 5:8, that you were once darkness, but now you are light in the Lord. Therefore, walk as children of light.

The Apostle Peter wrote that He has called us out of darkness into the marvelous light (1 Peter 2:9)! However, Peter wrote this verse in the context of the church becoming the new mediatorial agents of the covenant representing the Kingdom of God upon earth. They possess the keys to the Kingdom as a chosen generation, a royal priesthood, a holy nation, and God's special people for possession. The church is the new temporary assembly representing God's light in a dark world during the church age. We are recognized as

1 Precept Austin. *Luke 11 Commentary – The Pretense of Sight*, Retrieved from https://www.preceptaustin.org/luke-11-commentary

a people, not as a person; thus, we MUST physically gather. Our physical and visible gathering benefits the Kingdom, the church, the members of the church, and the world. People are being transformed by the power of the Kingdom through the witness of the church. The church is the light of God in a dark world. People cannot have a relationship with God without the light of the church. Thus, when John spoke of darkness, he was referring to the state of one's relationship with God. And when the state of the relationship is proper, then fellowship is established through walking in the truth (John 8:32).

If we "walk" (περιπατέω: *peripateó*, figuratively, of how one conducts one's daily life behave, live; with the dative to denote attendant circumstances, manner, and kind of life) in the light as He is in the "light" (φῶς: *phós*, φωτός: photos, as a religious metaphor, used especially of God as the ultimate source of light and of the sphere where he exists), we have fellowship with one another, and the blood of Jesus Christ His Son cleanses us from all sin (1 John 1:7). John suggests that through a relationship with Christ, we can have fellowship with

one another. And the blood cleanses us from ALL sin. God has provided us with a corporate salvation with individual responsibilities while we corporately gather to continue to be transformed through the process of sanctification. But if we say we have no sin, it is an indication that we are not walking in relationship or fellowship! Instead, we are being deceived in darkness due to the lack of walking in the light of the Word.

Paul wrote and instructed Timothy to "Pay attention to yourself and to the teaching, continue in it, for by so doing you will deliver both yourself and those who hear you" (1 Timothy 4:16). Whenever we gather for corporate worship, it is a time for reflective comparisons with God's Word. If we confess our sins, He is faithful and just to forgive us our sins and cleanse us from all unrighteousness or things that hinder the relationship. If we say we have not sinned, though, we make Him a liar, and His Word is not in us (1 John 1:9-10).

Thus, fellowship is based upon relationship. According to Jesus Himself, the greatest commandments are – you must love God with all your heart, soul, mind, and strength, and love your neighbor as yourself (Mark 12:30). Relationship with God places one in fellowship with God and establishes fellowship with man. God is always concerned about the vertical relationship between God and man and the horizontal relationship between people. Physical gathering is the furnace of spiritual refinement that shapes and molds one for the eternal gathering. Thus, fellowship with God is simply about love for God and His creation, light, which is walking in the truth of His Word, and life, which suggests that we are living the God-intended life in community!

11

PENTECOST AND THE POWER OF GATHERING

In this chapter, I want to specifically discuss Pentecost and the power of gathering. We are living in what I'm convinced are the last days. I believe that the generation that will usher in Christ and the rapture of the church may be alive. In the Olivet discourse, along with the Pauline and Petrine epistles, warning signs pronounce the activities and attitudes of the end-time church. We also have the prophetic utterances of Daniel and the Older Testament prophets concerning the end of days. The book of Revelation provides us with John's vision of the seven churches of Asia Minor, which represent the entire church age from beginning to end. According to biblical eschatology, all of the end-time prophecies have been fulfilled. The stage is being set for the Tribulation Period.

The end-time church age is characterized by the Laodicean church (Revelation 3:14-22). This Asia Minor church existed within a wealthy economic climate due to its phrygia powder or eye salve, black wool industry, and other economic advantages due to its location. Amid its economic prosperity, this end-time church has adopted a health and wealth mentality of independence because of its scientific breakthroughs in medicine, technology, and economics. The church boasts of being rich in increase and having need of nothing (Revelation 3:17). This end-time church's prosperity caused it to have the spirit of independence. The end time seventh church of Asia Minor is a church that is deceived; thus, it is both bound and blind (Revelation 3:17).

Christ's admonishment was to buy gold refined in the fire, which is an instruction to revisit their understanding of God, whose Son had to suffer for your redemption (Revelation 3:18). Then He admonished them to buy white clothes, which is symbolic of righteousness, to clothe the shame of their nakedness. Then, He advised them to get a covering, supplied by Christ, to cover the shame of their nakedness in ignorance. He also instructed them to get eye salve to apply to their spiritual eye disease so that they may see.

Christ then outlined His interaction with the church and said, "I rebuke and discipline everyone I love, so exert yourself and turn from your sins....here, I stand at the door, if anyone hears My voice and opens the door, I will come into him and eat with him, and he will sit and eat with Me. I will let him who wins the victory sit with Me on my throne, Just as I won the victory and sat down with My Father on His throne, let he that has an ear hear what the Spirit is saying to the church" (Revelation 3:19-22). Christ's explanation to the church suggests that the end-time church will have to rigorously deal with the spirit of independence and subjectivity.

The spirit of independence and subjectivity results from Satan capitalizing upon human subjectivity, which is derived from the reign of human DNA known as temperament, carnality, or flesh. Satan's strategy in the Garden of Eden caused Adam and Eve to lean to their own understanding. But the Bible states that a carnal mind is enmity with God (Romans

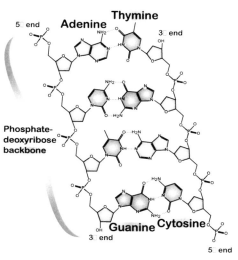

Chemical structure of DNA

8:7). Additionally, the Bible speaks of the consequence of doublemindedness and admonishes us to let that mind that was in Christ Jesus be also in us (Philippians 2:5). So the end-time church must contend with human subjectivity due to the departure from the faith and giving over to seducing spirits and doctrines of demons (1 Timothy 4:1). This has taken place over time by watering down the gospel and polluting it with watershed theology (Romanization, Europeanization, Colonization, Westernization, and Americanization of the gospel).

The second ploy of Satan is independence – the desire to not need anything or anybody, which is a deceptive attack of pride. Pride leads to both isolation and independence. Satan makes us feel that we can exist spiritually in isolation. However, we were created with the DNA of community; Eve was inside Adam when humanity was created. Later, God stated that it is not good for man to be alone (Genesis 2:18). Satan attacked Eve when she was alone and capitalized on her misunderstanding (she stated God said don't touch when He did not say that) and innocence (Satan is a liar) in order to gain an advantage. Satan does his best work in isolation, and God does His best work in community. This is why post-COVID will be one of the most challenging hours for the Christian church. We will have to try and make a comeback from social distancing and online church for over a year.

There is Power in Community!	
A threefold cord is not easily broken	Ecclesiastes 4:12
Where two or three gather together in His name, there He will be in the midst of them	Matthew 18:19
One can chase a thousand but two ten thousand	Deuteronomy 32:30
What I'm getting at is that there is power in gathering!	

When God established His covenant with Israel, He did not send Moses around with a petition for them to sign; He assembled them (*qahal*). It was a part of the protocols of the Kingdom – to gather in order to receive an impartation from God. Israel gathered at the blowing of the shofar for worship, weddings, war, and wise counsel. While most people would not disagree with the necessity of gathering philosophically, they would debate how we meet. When it comes to the church and the covenant community of God, there is always an attachment to a physical place.

Long distance can only last so long. During the COVID-19 pandemic, I listened to one of my congregants' graduations from medical school, and the young man who gave the commencement speech discussed his struggle with getting into medical school. When he finally got accepted, it was 5 hours away from the love of his life. So he decided that his relationship with her would be disrupted and possibly destroyed being five hours away. So he believed God, and long to short, and got accepted to the University of Texas in Galveston. He understood the value of gathering; long-distance relationships can only last so long until you need a touch. He understood that certain things could not be accomplished at a distance. As I listened to him and thought about the church and prolonged social distancing, I thought about what can be lost if we separate too long. And as I predicted, many people no longer value physical gathering.

The call to worship in the Bible is a corporate call, and certain things only happen when we gather corporately, which involves a physical space. God has always required a physical place for worship, as mentioned earlier. For Adam, it was the garden; for Noah, it was the ark; for Abram, it was the place God would show him; for Moses and Israel, it was the Tabernacle; for David, it was Jerusalem; for Solomon, it was the Temple; for the exilic Jews, it was the synagogue (which required a minyan); for Jesus, it was the house of prayer not a den of thieves; for the early church, it was the Temple and the house; for the patristics and the catholic church, it was the basilica; for Roman Catholics, it is the cathedral; and for Protestants, it is the church. The work of God, which is evangelism and discipleship, requires physical gathering, because the church, governed by the fivefold ministry, as mentioned in Ephesians 4:11 and 1 Corinthians 12:28, is the pillar and ground of truth (1 Timothy 3:15).

Nothing replaces physical gathering and the church's power when it gathers. During times of social, political, and economic crisis, people turn to the church. During the world wars, they turned to the church; during Vietnam, they turned to the church; in past pandemics, they turned to the church; and after the September 11, 2001 attack on America, church attendance increased because people,  once again, turned to the church. While it takes, sometimes, an act of war or a national crisis to cause people to turn to the church, the church is the ultimate voice, representing God on earth. Historically, it has been the source of calm and safety in our world and society. Even concerning political issues, the church is considered an asylum or sanctuary; in other words, it is off-limits. The church and its physical gathering have been the calming power of the world. Without the gathering of the church, chaos and destruction take place, as revealed in the Tribulation Period, because of the absence of the physical church.

When we gather and not scatter, we represent the authority of God's Word and voice to the world. We represent the embassy of Christ and His Kingdom on foreign soil. We represent political power when we gather; our collective votes assist in upholding the values of our faith. When we gather, we represent economic power and social presence. When we gather, we represent the conscience of God among the heathenistic attitudes of the world. When we gather, we represent a visible force that must be reckoned with. Thus, united we stand and divided we fall.

How vital is gathering, and at what expense should the church gather today? Today, in our nation, we have been facing the horror of the novel coronavirus, known as COVID-19. This virus has killed over 600,000 U.S. lives alone, not to mention more than 4 million deaths worldwide. This virus has been deemed as possibly one of the most contagious and deadliest viruses known to man. Our country was on lockdown for almost a year with stay-home or shelter-in-place orders to adhere to the Center for Disease Control's strategy of contagion mitigation. There was political and journalistic warfare between CNN and the White House during the Trump administration concerning social distancing in light of the President and his party's desire to re-open the economy. This deadly pandemic changed both our behavior and our hearts.

The pandemic revealed some more ugly truths about the American health system. African Americans suffered an extremely high loss of life from COVID-19 for various reasons associated with the inequity of access to health and economics in the country. This discovery came to light while the community faced the unjust losses of African American lives at the hands of law enforcement. The death of George Floyd tipped the pot of social injustice and unrest and sparked fierce protests around the world. Thousands gathered from all over the nation – some peaceful, some not peaceful, protesting the death of blacks at the hands and knees of white police officers. People gathered around the country, during a pandemic, for a cause. George Floyd's death by suffocation under the knee of the Minneapolis police was recorded live. The world, horrified, watched as a white police officer snuffed the life out of a handcuffed and subjugated 46-year-old black man who was not resisting arrest. This outrage sparked protestors who gathered by the thousands, shoulder to shoulder and side by side, not regarding the rules of social distancing. Why? Because their cause was greater than their risk. They placed themselves in jeopardy to death by cop, crowd, and COVID-19. However, it did not stop them from gathering. Why? Because they understood the power of mass gatherings; when you do not gather, you cannot be heard.

The church must take a note out of the pages of these protesters, which include every ethnic persuasion, generation, and social class. The church is afraid to gather because of risk, and this is because there is no cause! I heard one person say they are not going back to church for the remainder of the year and others saying that they are just going to stream from here on out. The problem is that' church folks' are not Kingdom-minded; they have no cause. I understand how we must engage in responsible re-gathering, but sports arenas and other large crowd venues have reconvened while the church continues to disregard the significance of the physical gathering.

Additionally, many of our church members attend other types of secular gatherings, including vacations crowded with people, airplane travel, and restaurants, to mention a few. I know that the streaming lifestyle has become comfortable for both the pastor and the pew, however, as the assembly, we must physically gather as the embassy of God on foreign soil. If the church doesn't re-emerge soon, she will potentially lose the presence power that Christ established for us.

According to recent research, almost 8,000 church-es a year closed in the decade ending in 2020, which is about 150 congregations per week.[1] After the pan-demic, the numbers are expected to double or triple to almost 24,000 churches closing per year, never to open their doors again. This phenomenon diminishes the church's geo-graphical footprint and presence. The church is the most powerful entity in minority commu-nities, and we risk our power because of our fear. In con-trast, minority pro-testors gathered in record numbers without fear of con-sequence because they had a cause. Gathering might pose a danger, but the threat of losing the presence and power of the church in the world is a greater cause, making the risk worthwhile. Thus, we have to gather responsibly.

More Protestant churches closed than started in 2019

Estimates based on information from 34 denominational and other groups representing 60% of U.S. Protestant churches

2019 — 3,000 openings / 4,500 closures

2014 — 4,000 openings / 3,700 closures

Lifeway research

Source: Lifeway Research estimates of 2019 Protestant church starts and closures based on unofficial reports gathered from 34 denominational groups that represent 60% of U.S. Protestant churches

While shallow people will relegate physical gathering to some economic benefits, I have argued the theo-logical and biblical reasons why we gather in this

---

1 Religion News Service. *Study: More Churches Closing Than Opening*, Retrieved from https://religionnews.com/2021/05/26/study-more-church-es-closing-than-opening/

book. In a nutshell, there simply is no church if there is no gathering. We are a community of individuals, not an individual community. Certain things happen only when the faith community gathers that allows us to sustain our spiritual lives and presence in perpetuity, which cannot occur outside of gathering.

Let's consider Pentecost, the birth of the physically gathered church. Pre-Pentecost, Jesus commanded the disciples to gather in the upper room after finding them gathered in a house with the doors locked (Luke 24:49). A quick read of the Pentecost narrative may cause you to miss the fear that gripped the disciples because of the controversial death of Christ. The Romans and the Jews pursued His followers due to the potential of religious division. Upon the crucifixion of Christ, the disciples were hiding for their lives. Under that pressure, Peter denied Jesus three times, just as Jesus prophesied. Locked away and hiding, this was possibly the first model of social distancing; Peter was on lockdown and in isolation.

However, after the resurrection, Christ paid all of the disciples a physical visit, because some things cannot be done at a distance. The disciples became inundated with the restoration of a political and economic kingdom that would fulfill the Older Testament prophecies of the Messiah. But Jesus redirected their immediate focus to the coming of power not many days henceforth (Acts 1:8). Luke, the physician and writer of the book of Acts and the gospel, detailed that Christ instructed His disciples to gather in Jerusalem until they were clothed with power from on high. Luke wrote that they were all gathered together in the upper room (Acts 2:1). Thus, we discover that before God gave the gift of the Holy Spirit, He commanded a group of people (120) to a certain place (upper room).

The context of this narrative is the Feast of Weeks or Pentecost, which follows the Feast of Passover, Unleavened Bread, and Firstfruits. This is one of the busiest seasons of the seven feasts following firstfruits. The people have presented their firstfruits to God, and upon Him receiving them, the harvest began. It took seven weeks to gather in the harvest; the fruit was ready, and then the olives were gathered. The vineyards became hives of activity with the vintage (the process of picking grapes and producing wine). The season began with barley but concluded with the ingathering of wheat.

The Feast of Pentecost is also known as Shavuot or Weeks (שָׁבוּעַ) (Exodus 34:22, Deuteronomy 16:10, 2 Chronicles 8:13). The feast was celebrated in late May-early June. The feast was referred to by three designations that pointed out different aspects of meanings of the feast.

- The Feast of Weeks points out the time

- The Day of Firstfruits (Numbers 28:26)

- The Feast of Harvest (Exodus 23:16)

Pentecost was the official day of the beginning of the summer harvest. It was a time of grand celebration and a special journey to Jerusalem. Leviticus 23:15-16 states that from the day after the Sabbath from the Feast of Firstfruits, count seven full weeks, and then you shall offer a new grain offering to the Lord. The Feast of Pentecost marked the beginning of the summer harvest. During the Feast of Pentecost, many more crops were available than at Firstfruits. However, the fall harvest would produce the most. Pentecost occurs on a Sunday, because it must follow a sabbath (Leviticus 23:15-

16). Pentecost occurs exactly 50 days after Firstfruits. The Jews celebrated this feast with two loaves of leavened bread that represented that the church would comprise of both Jews and Gentiles.

Pentecost by Julius Schnorr von Carolsfeld

The Day of Pentecost produced a great harvest of 3,000 souls, which speaks to Exodus 32:28, referring to when Moses threw the tablets on the golden calf; 3,000 died that day. This was not a coincidence; the letter kills, but the Spirit gives life! He was crucified on Passover, buried on Unleavened Bread, raised on Firstfruits, and the Holy Spirit was sent on Pentecost. The harvest of Pentecost was the harvest of souls. The Bible states they were added to the church, not that they were the church. Pentecost created a new people for God, a new assembly that represented His presence among the nations – the church.

Three commands of Pentecost (Deuteronomy 16:9-12) required, in the natural, that those gathered for the feast, as prescribed by God Himself, were to:

1. Release a Seed! A free-will offering not presented on the altar but waved by the priest forward, backward, up then down, then eaten in the festive meal by the priest later (Leviticus 23:20)
2. Rejoice before the Lord (whole family or network)
3. Remember your salvation experience

In 140 AD, the Sanhedrin convened and changed the focus of Shavuot from an agricultural feast to the giving of the law at Sinai. The law was also given in the third month, so they attached it to the feast to celebrate the giving of the law in Judaism.

Pentecost was a great experience that led to a supernatural explosion by the prophetic clock of God. Thus, God and His new creation, the church, were situated in physical gathering for His use, because certain things can only occur in a physical gathering. I have been in ministry for over 36 years, and I have brought thousands of people to Christ. I have prayed for thousands of people and seen thousands of miracles, but 99%+ of these experiences happened in the corporate gathering. An anointing resides in the sanctuary and physical gathering that cannot be duplicated or replaced by any other environment.

There is a power released for salvation, miracles, healing, and deliverance that only takes place in physical gatherings. This is one of the reasons why I believe the psalter was so appreciative of the opportunity to go into God's house for worship, "I was glad when they said unto me, let us go into the house of the Lord"

(Psalm 122:1). The psalter was excited, not simply about himself going into the house but "us" going in. The summons into the house of the Lord was based upon God inviting them; the proper response – Let us go! This text suggests that something very powerful happens when we are physically gathered with expectation. You cannot get at home what you get in a physical gathering. That doesn't mean that God cannot touch you through technology, but nothing substitutes and replaces physical gathering.

Pentecost or gatherings produced the following:	
1.	There was a sound: we hear the voice of God and the power of the Spirit.
2.	There was a sitting: a posture of listening and waiting for experience and explanation. Prayer!
3.	There was a seeing: we get vision in our gatherings
4.	There was empowerment to speak: the Spirit rested upon them, and they spoke by the Spirit – wind and fire, blowing and passion, direction and power to move!

Things happen when we gather that don't happen if we are not gathered. There is power in Pentecost or Holy Spirit-filled gatherings.

12 THE ONLINE CHURCH CHALLENGE

With the global pandemic, one must ask how has church online impacted the church – its leaders and laymen? How has the church fared in the transition to being a digital church? Has online church been effective in providing the necessary spiritual empowerment required for spiritual growth and development? In this chapter, I want to take a look at what early research is showing concerning many churches returning to in-person services.

As the thesis of this book has demonstrated, the people of God are a people in physical gatherings. The Christian church began in a physical gathering in the upper room where 120 believers were instructed by the Messiah to gather and wait for the outpouring of the Holy Spirit. The scriptures are replete with passages that demonstrate that God's people have historically, through biblical mandate, participated in physical gatherings. The early church was a multicultural and multilingual gathering, which encompassed all of the nations of the world – people from the continents of Africa, Asia, and Europe who heard the disciples preach in their native languages.

Most of the 1st century believers were Jewish who gathered in homes, catacombs, and any place that was suitable and safe for gathering. After the destruction of the Temple in 70 AD by Emperor Titus, the gathering rituals of the Jewish people were hindered from going there, but the Gentile believers continued to gather in homes. "Christian gathering as seen from Church history appears to have foundations in the theological, sociological, and cultural orientation of the early church irrespective of where the faith was proclaimed."[1]

In the article, "Social Distance Impact on Church Gatherings: Socio-Behavioral Implications" by Taylor & Francis Online, the following was listed as the theological significance of religious gathering:[2]

> "First, from a theological standpoint, the church defined as ekklesia connotes the gathering of the called-out ones (Zizioulas, 2002). The gathering means being bound or bonded together as one body in communion with Christ through the agent of the Holy Spirit. Others have argued that this gathering does not necessarily refer to the physical congregating at a location (church and unchurched folks on social media). Subsequently, there were several occasions where the physical gathering of other congregants triggered a pneumatic experience (Acts 4:23-31; 5:12-16; 13:1-5). In addition to these, the first evangelistic min-

1 Taylor & Francis Online. *Social distance impact on church gatherings...*
https://www.tandfonline.com/doi/full/10.1080/10911359.2020.1793869
2 Ibid.

istry of Peter where 3,000 people were added to the church, Luke recorded that "All that believed were together and had all things in common" (Acts 2:44). Finally, the author of Hebrews admonished Christ's adherents, "Not forsaking the assembling of ourselves together, as the manner of some is, but exhorting one another; and so much the more as you see the day approaching" (Hebrews 10:25). Theologically, the Bible emphasizes the importance of Christian gathering and it is imperative for them to congregate for various reasons and religious functions."

Snyder writes, "The church is a community with social nexus and cultural values. In his redemptive work, Jesus creates a new, reconciled community where Jews and Gentiles meet as sisters and brothers in one peaceable family" (Snyder, 2001).[3] Alikin posits that "This view lends credence to Christian gathering as the conduit of social connection and sharing common values. Meeting in the synagogue on the Sabbath to engage in activities such as reading, praying, singing, eating, and preaching, although a Jewish religious event, are all part of Christian gathering practice" (Alikin, 2010).[4] He further postulates:

"that such practices are embedded in the customs of both Jewish and Graeco-Roman philosophical beliefs. The early church, which began

3 Ibid.
4 Ibid.

in this socio-cultural milieu, adopted these activities as part of their social connections and values within a biblical context. The early church perceived themselves, regardless of their location and persecution, as a community that could not be segregated. Is this perception of community or Christian gathering practice applicable to the contemporary church irrespective of their socio-cultural environment or during adverse conditions? While the early church interpreted physical gathering as a spiritual rite, duty and obligation there are those who feel as though it is an option."[5]

The article also states:

"Others have argued that Christian gathering is of no importance, considering the havoc the COVID-19 virus is unleashing, since the church is a spiritual entity and worshipping via online transmission is not different from congregating. While these arguments are tenable and meant to preserve lives of parishioners, a cursory examination of Christian gathering from a socio-theological and cultural perspectives make these issues debatable. During these times when a moratorium is placed on churches, community building, social connections and attitudinal changes are being hampered. No doubt, the American Psychological Association (APA) has observed that the lockdown has triggered depression, anxiety disorders and adverse behavioral changes to the American people (American Psychological Association, 2020)."[6]

---

5 Ibid.
6 Ibid.

It is the position of many that churches should be allowed to open and follow the guidelines of other organizations, but denying physical gathering has taken a negative toll on people. It is noted that COVID-19 has taken lives in all environments, including the health sector. However, African Americans or black people have traditionally worked in the hourly, low-wage employment sector in retail trades, personal and laundry services, maids and housekeepers, and food services. They are also less likely than others to work from home to follow social distancing due to both a lack of digital and financial resources (Gupta et al., 2019; De Silver, 2020). Hence, as frontline workers in nursing homes, hospitals, food service workers, and janitors (Stabenow & Schumer, 2020), they hesitantly risk being infected by COVID-19 because they are less likely to have paid sick days and paid family and medical leave that would allow them to remain at home during the epidemic (Gupta et al., 2019). Therefore, many Black and low-income people still go to work and risk being infected by COVID-19 as a matter of economic survival.[7] While church gathering, at some point, posed a potential danger, other segments of the population, like African Americans who were dying at alarming rates, were being totally neglected.

The article discussed the physiological deficiency that occurred and its effects upon people due to social distancing. The author writes, "Being touched can be a powerful experience. For the purpose of this discussion, the authors will discuss social touch that is nonsexual in relation to social distancing. Of all sensory modalities, touch is the earliest to develop and functions as a "sensory scaffold on which we come to perceive our own bodies and our sense of self" (Bremner & Spence,

---

7 Ibid.

2017).[8] It has been found that social touch, when given to comfort a loved one who is in pain, produces biological alterations that are related to empathy (Cascio et al., 2019). Touch is often used to transmit emotions between individuals. For those in intimate relationships, touch can facilitate pain relief (Goldstein et al., 2017).[9]

In light of the current chaotic state of both this nation and the world, people need and desire social touch (Von Mohr et al., 2017). Social touch is an integral part of the Christian faith-based experience. In many religious institutions, there are a plethora of opportunities for tactile interactions. For instance, people may be greeted with a hug by ushers and/or designated greeters as they enter their church. During the time that may be set aside to acknowledge visitors, congregants may be asked to stand to shake hands with the visitor(s) and with each other. Sometimes, at the close of the religious experience, while the congregants hold hands, the church leader may pray a benediction over them.

Additionally, it is not uncommon for a pastor, priest, or other church leaders to interact with members of the congregation with a handshake before they leave the facility. That can be a meaningful gesture in that a touch can be reassuring to people who are alone,

8 Bremner, Andrew; Spence, Charles. *The Development of Tactile Perception*, https://www.researchgate.net/publication/313541882_The_Development_of_Tactile_Perception
9 Taylor & Francis Online. *Social distance impact on church gatherings...*

afraid, hurting, and anxious (Sin & Koole, 2013).[10] When we look at social distancing for prolonged periods and its effects on the masses, we see that social distancing carries mental health issues within it.

Churches had to become very innovative in providing a sense of touch to their members, such as drive-in communion, drive-in church, and drive-in revivals. However, churches had to make quick adjustments as the order to shelter-in-place was given about three weeks before Easter. Congregations had to quickly shift to the utilization of technology to continue their worship services and ministry. This adjustment began a change in how religious services were to be offered for the next year and a half. "Just 20% of the congregations streamed their services, and 48% had the ability to accept donations electronically before the pandemic (Boorstein, 2020)." "The shift from face-to-face worship to "virtual" services provided an opportunity for congregations to reimagine their presence beyond their sanctuary, a specific geographic location, and their current membership base."[11]

Duke Divinity scholar Gregory Jones (2016) reminds us of John Gardner's timeless and life-giving approach to innovation:[12]

> Every individual, organization or society must mature, but much depends on how this maturing takes place. A society whose maturing consists of simply acquiring more firmly established ways of doing things is headed for the graveyard – even if it learns to do things with greater and greater skill. In the ever-renewing society what matures is a system or framework within which

10 Ibid.
11 Ibid.
12 Ibid.

continuous innovation, renewal and rebirth can occur (p. 2).

During this season, the church had to re-present its ministry to the congregation and to the world, utilizing a totally different approach to express its witness of Christ to the world.

> "Many congregations are beginning to move toward the innovation and renewal necessary to maintain the vitality of their congregations. These congregations let go of their former format to adapt to current circumstances and focus on their future. This pandemic has opened the way for innovations including new technologies to preserve worship service and ministries; adaptation of spiritual practices and ministries as well as rekindling of relationships among family, friends, congregations, other institutions, and across cities."[13]

As congregations had to close and cancel in-person gatherings, they rushed to Facebook, Facebook Live, Zoom, Skype, Instagram, YouTube, giving apps, conference lines, and live streaming to continue their primary worship services, other services, community ministries, and even concerts (Burke, 2020; Trepany, 2020).[14]

Research conducted revealed the following: A Gallup poll found that 19% of Americans interviewed between March 28 to April 1, 2020 reported that "their faith or spirituality has gotten better as a result of the crisis, while three percent say it has gotten worse" (Newport, 2020). Pew Research Center found a similar trend. In particular, Americans attending historically Black churches and those that self-identify as very religious—

13 Ibid.
14 Ibid.

those that frequently pray and attend services—are most likely to report that their faith has strengthened (Gecewicz, 2020).[15] Without getting too involved in the implications of health-related issues stemming from COVID-19, it is clear that the lack of gathering had a significant impact upon both church members and church leaders.

The Impact of COVID Upon the Post-COVID Church

While only 36% of people on average have returned back to church since the moratorium has been lifted on attendance, based on a Barna church study, it reported that "Half of Churched Adults Have Not Streamed a Church Service in the Past Four Weeks." The majority of pastors (96%) say their churches have been streaming their worship services online during the pandemic. But that may not matter for nearly half of churched adults—that is, those who say they have attended church in the past six months. Forty-eight

percent of this group report they have not streamed an online service in the last month. Even looking at a more consistent segment—practicing Christians, who are typically characterized by at least monthly attendance—one in three (32%) admit they have not streamed an online service during this time.[16]

When we rely upon streaming as the main avenue of worship due to the initial effect it had

---

15 Ibid.
16 Barna.com. State of the Church - What Research Has Revealed About the New Sunday Morning …. https://www.barna.com/research/new-sunday-morning/

during the onset of social distancing, we do not understand the church's new challenge. People are no longer committed to streaming as they were in the beginning. Researchers were surprised to see this seeming dip among regular attenders, particularly considering that a plurality of Protestant pastors (40%) had reported increased virtual attendance since the pandemic pushed services online. Additionally, weekend schedules during the crisis have likely looked more open. Many churches now offer on-demand streaming after an initial service or upload; 29 percent of practicing Christians and 20 percent of non-practicing Christians say they take advantage of this option on a day other than Sunday. These are all reasons virtual attendance could have been boosted, but it's possible that enthusiasm for only online service options has dwindled as the weeks have passed.[17]

One of the challenges that the online church is facing is the issue of commitment to a single church. Church members are dividing their loyalty to multiple churches they stream. Churched adults logging in for services usually opt for their regular church home (40%). However, 23 percent have streamed services from a different church, essentially "church-hopping" online. One-third of practicing Christians (34% vs. 16% non-practicing Christians) have also virtually attended a church other than their own in the past month. In-

17 Ibid.

deed, we see one-quarter of practicing Christians (26% vs. 12% non-practicing Christians) notes that, during the pandemic, this has become typical of their online attendance. This seems to be pre-COVID-19 attendance habits, as 35 percent of churched adults and 26 percent of practicing Christians told us in December 2019 that they usually divide their attendance among two or more churches.[18] The online streaming option provides church members a way to not be committed to a church, nor its covering or community.

Another challenge of online church is that research shows 15% of practicing Christians multitask while streaming worship services. What does the new Sunday morning look like for Christian households who continue to tune in to virtual worship services? Does the level of attentiveness change when a household is streaming the message in a living room or bedroom instead of following the motions of a group of people gathered in a physical building?[19] While some research suggests that many have a challenge paying attention to in-person worship, it is usually based on personal spirituality. Practicing and non-practicing Christians have different routines during online services. For example, while three in five practicing Christians (64%) say they still pray along with prayers, only two in five non-practicing Christians (41%) say the same. This trend is similar for other practices, such as households watching services together at the same time (42% practicing Christians vs. 21% non-practicing Christians) or singing along with worship (40% vs. 23%). Many churchgoers also admit that attending online services offers an opportunity for them to multitask while the service is streaming (15% practicing Christians vs. 30% non-practicing Christians).[20]

---

18 Ibid.
19 Ibid.
20 Ibid.

Despite being one of the necessary gifts provided by God to the church, the spiritual leader or five-fold ministry gift that watches and feeds the believer with knowledge and understanding, people are still not coming due to the development of poor habits. Just three in ten churchgoers have had contact with a church leader in the last month. In a time of social distancing and isolation—something that is impacting the relational, emotional, and mental health of both pastors and their people—the level of connection among churched adults is suffering. Relational measures of participation, at least, are low. For example, while it may be the norm to have a quick chat with your pastor on a Sunday morning, only 30 percent of practicing Christians and 4 percent of non-practicing Christians say they've had contact with their church leader within the last month. Additionally, only 15 percent of practicing Christians (and just 3% of non-practicing Christians) have joined a prayer meeting online in the past four weeks. Even lower numbers met with a small group or Bible study (12% practicing vs. 3% non-practicing).[21]

While the Bible instructs the believer to imitate their leader and to obey and submit to their spiritual authority because they are watching out for you, people are not connecting with their spiritual leaders. The church of Laodicea lost her covering and was naked and ashamed. It is crucial to connect with your spiritual leader based on the Word of God. However, currently two in five practicing Christians (42%) and one in 10 non-practicing Christians (8%) say they have listened to or watched a message from a religious leader of any type online in the past four weeks. Others say they have searched for spiritual answers online (11% vs.

---

21 Ibid.

7%) or found some other way of practicing faith online (8% vs. 4%).[22]

It is clear that social distancing has had a tremendous impact on the attitudes and practices of church members in terms of frequency and engagement. Recent data shows that among practicing Christians—those who identify as Christian agree strongly that faith is very important in their lives and attend church at least monthly (prior to COVID-19). Over half (53%) say they have streamed their regular church online within the past four weeks. Another 34 percent admits to streaming a different church service online other than their own, essentially "church hopping" digitally. Finally, about one-third of practicing Christians (32%) say they have done neither of these things. One in three practicing Christians have neither streamed their pre-COVID church nor streamed another church's service. Though some of these churchgoers may be part of the minority of congregations that were still gathering for physical worship during these weeks, we can, for the

---

22 Ibid.

most part, confidently interpret this group as those who have dropped out of church for the time being.[23]

Those that were a part of the research concerning the last four weeks of worship participation post-COVID stated that over four weeks, they streamed both their church's online service and a different church's service, perhaps taking advantage of the variety and surge of digital options. However, the plurality has stayed tuned in to their "home" church even at home. When looking for practicing Christians who are still and only attending their pre-COVID-19 church, we find that just over a third (35%) say this has been their course of action. Commitment extends to the frequency of attendance during distancing as well; practicing Christians who stream the same church they attended before COVID-19 are significantly more likely than those who have switched churches to attend on a weekly basis (81% vs. 65%).[24]

Research is showing that people are also switching churches, moving past their pre-COVID churches. However, those who have streamed their church faithfully are more prone to stay with their churches, though it may impact their in-person participation and attendance. We see that very few (14%) have actually made a church switch amid the pandemic. It is more likely for a Christian to have stopped attending church altogether during the pandemic; in fact, 32 percent of practicing Christians have done just that. The remaining 18% of practicing Christians are viewing worship services from multiple churches throughout the month.

23 Barna.com. *State of the Church - One in Three Practicing Christians Has Stopped Attending* …. https://www.barna.com/research/new-sunday-morning-part-2/
24 Ibid.

The research also reveals that the church is having an intergenerational challenge in reaching the next generation. In the article, "Half of Practicing Christian Millennials Are Not Viewing Services Online," a profile of these groups of online churchgoers reveals a strong generational pattern. When asked if they had attended church within the past four weeks, exactly half of practicing Christian Millennials (50%) say they have not. The percentages of Gen X and Boomers who have stopped attending online services (35% Gen X, 26% Boomers) are lower than among their younger counterparts, but still show the impact of COVID-19 precautions and regulations on what used to be a regular practice. Though younger generations might be more accustomed to digital routines and innovations, their tenuous relationship with institutions seems to persist during this era of the digital church. These trends highlight the importance of churches continuing to reach out to and disciple the next generation, especially those who are seemingly falling away during the pandemic.[25]

Research is also continuing to display the negative emotional effects that the lack of in-person church triggered among multiple generations. The article, "Those No Longer Attending Church Bear More Emotional Burdens," states that among practicing Christians who have lessened or completely stopped digital worship attendance, individual flourishing—a term we apply to new research-backed metrics church leaders can use to encourage spiritual and personal growth among their people—is also hindered based on Barna data. This can be observed, for example, in the way respondents answer questions related to certain emotions. Respondents who have stopped attending church during COVID-19 are less likely than their peers,

25 Ibid.

who are still attending the same church during the pandemic, to agree with the statement, "I am not anxious about my life, as I have an inner peace from God" (76% vs. 87%). Practicing Christians who have stopped attending church in recent weeks are more likely than all other practicing Christians to say they feel bored "all of the time" (17% vs. 6%) or that they have felt "insecure" for at least some of each day (11% vs. 7%).[26]

While research doesn't show causations, it reveals correlations; thus, we can only predict behaviors based upon correlation. Indicators demonstrate that people who are not a part of a congregation tend to have a more challenging emotional life than those who are. What we do know is that churchgoers, even those who have stopped regularly attending worship services during the pandemic, want support from a church community. Practicing Christians across the U.S. are seeking "prayer and emotional support" (68% who have moved churches during COVID-19, 52% who have stayed at their same church) and "a Bible-centered message of hope and encouragement" (44% who have stayed at their same church, 35% of all other practicing Christians) from their churches.[27] I hope that this data helps you see the negative impact and challenges that online worship alone has had on some people. In the last chapter, let's explore how we can make online worship work in a hybrid church context.

---

26 Ibid.
27 Ibid.

13 PHYSICAL GATHERING, DISRUPTION, AND ONLINE CHURCH

COVID-19 was and is a game-changer for many industries; it was a time of disruption. Disruption is defined as "the act or process of disrupting something: a break or interruption in the normal course or continuation of some activity, process, etc." It is a major disturbance, something that changes your plans or interrupts some event or process. A screaming child on an airplane can be a disruption of the passengers' sleep.[1] For the church, COVID-19 was a disruption.

---

1 Vocabulary.com. *Disruption* - Dictionary Definition, Retrieved from https://www.vocabulary.com/dictionary/disruption

2020 was a year that many churches decided they would focus on their church's vision. Almost every church on the planet went with the theme of "20/20," which I believe was natural and organic. Church leaders had tremendously high hopes of leading their congregations into a year of high performance and expectation. This year only comes around once, and many placed a high level of expectation on the move of the Holy Spirit and the power of God to help the church rally around the concept of biblical vision. Some leaders had high hopes and expectations for using the year 2020 to focus on bringing their fledgling visions vitality and vigor. I was among these church leaders who saw a tremendous opportunity to take advantage of this once-in-a-lifetime chance to organically move people towards living a focused life for the Kingdom. This seemed to be a God-opportunity to lead the church back to the Bible basics of evangelism and discipleship. Not only was the year 2020 a gift for church leaders, but it was also the beginning of a decade. I referred to it as the "decade of champions." The year 2020 was full of hope, optimism, expectation, and opportunity, and many of us were ready to ride it until the wheels fell off.

The first month of the year 2020 was going well, then we experienced the tragic death of Kobe Bryant, which shook the world. Kobe Bryant was a multi-million-dollar Millennial who seemingly had nothing left to do in life but figure out how he would use his wealth to create new platforms to enjoy his hobbies and spend time with his daughters and wife. His very violent helicopter accident, in which he and his young daughter, along with several others, plunged to a horrific death, caused the world to mourn. Kobe's death impacted multiple continents and classes of people, including church leaders. This event was the focus of every news channel nationwide, and the conversation that the whole world was having in utter amazement. How could someone so young, so rich, and with every reason to live die like this? And to top it off, he died on a Sunday morning, the day of worship. Unbelievable! I remember when I heard the news right after church had ended; I was in utter disbelief, not Kobe.

While many professional athletes, coaches, and the entertainment industry were trying to wrap their minds around a reality that was disruptive for them, families, cultures, and generations were emotionally stung. This event made us look at life differently; it demonstrated that money, talent, potential, and fame cannot defeat the reality of death and mortality. Right on the heels of this wake-up call concerning mortality, when we just witnessed some of our toughest athletes and coaches losing it on national television over the death of the beloved Kobe Bryant, something more disruptive had already begun in Wuhan, China: the novel coronavirus. Unbeknownst to us, the novel coronavirus had already reached Europe and America in 2020. In what seemed like a year of opportunity and celebration, disruption began on the eve of 2020.

2020 ushered in the rise of the novel coronavirus, known as COVID-19. This very deadly virus attacks the respiratory system and several other organs, quickly leading to death or long-term health issues. 2020 literally began with a breathtaking virus that spread across the globe, taking thousands and thousands of lives from every race, gender, and class, regardless of where you resided. COVID-19 disrupted life worldwide and is still taking lives all over the world. As of July 9, 2021, the outbreak of the coronavirus disease (COVID-19) had spread to six continents, and almost four million people had died after contracting the respiratory virus.[2] America has suffered the most deaths of any other country in the world (620,000+) based upon research. The elderly and the African American community tend to be in the highest risk category due to underlying health issues, chronic diseases, and lower access to health care rooted in discriminatory practices.

The disease is still spreading. Testing has increased, but the deaths continue. The world is far from eradicating this virus. The health care system is still overwhelmed, and the health care professionals are extremely exhausted. While vaccines have entered the equation, so have new strands of the virus (variants). The vaccine is becoming less and less effective over time, creating global chaos. We are experiencing a disruption that I believe is crying out for effective and wise Kingdom leadership as the kingdoms of this world crumble under the irony of natural chaos and political and religious failure.

The most reliable alternative to slow this dreadful virus down was the practice of social distancing. Social distancing is a set of actions taken to stop or slow the

2 Statista.com. *Coronavirus deaths worldwide by country,* https://www.statista.com/statistics/1093256/novel-coronavirus-2019ncov-deaths-worldwide-by-country/

spread of a highly contagious disease. The goal of social distancing is to limit face-to-face contact and decrease the spread of illness among people in community settings.[3] The expected benefit of social distancing, aside from slowing and reducing the spread of illness, is to give the health care system a patient load it can manage. There must be adequate respirators, beds, PPE, etc., to effectively handle the highly contagious virus.

Social distancing changed our world. In 2020, for the first time in my lifetime, all sports events were discontinued for the season. At every educational level — college, high school, and elementary — the schools were closed, students were ordered to go home, and children had to learn online. All graduations were canceled due to social distancing, and all places of entertainment were ordered to close their businesses. Bowling alleys, theaters, theme parks, arcades, bars, and malls were ordered to close their doors. The CDC provided social distancing guidelines that were to be followed by everyone. While the essential businesses were allowed to offer goods and services to the public,

3 University of Utah Health. *Coronavirus (COVID-19) FAQs*, https://health-care.utah.edu/healthfeed/postings/2020/03/covid19-faqs.php

they had to modify how they served people; for example, restaurants could only provide to-go orders. Retail stores that were considered essential had to ensure that clientele remained six feet apart. Stores limited how many people could be served at a time in order to keep in compliance with CDC guidelines for social distancing. Non-essential businesses were asked to work from home and run their business at a distance and ordered to close their doors.

In Texas, during the shutdown, the church was classified as non-essential but allowed to offer its services online. The church being ordered to shut its doors was unprecedented and met with some resistance; however, the vast majority of us complied. While everyone knows that Easter is the most celebrated holy day of the Christian calendar, the church was online beginning at the Vatican and continued to the Protestant churches. This was a major societal disrupter! We provided our Resurrection Sunday worship services online in 2020 at a time when the pandemic was still spreading and threatening the lives of millions. Yet, people could not go to the one place that they historically could find comfort – the church or the house of God.

The whole world was experiencing disruption and the inability to continue business as usual; everyone had to modify organizational offerings to survive the pandemic.

COVID-19 disrupted the normal patterns and ecclesiastical industry of religious church services. For almost a year, the Christian church had to deliver all of its spiritual services through streaming networks and Zoom. With schools, major businesses, travel, and churches disrupted, domestic violence rates rose, and suicide rates rose; we experienced interpersonal relationship challenges due to this disruption. Our world has changed, and we, as humans, are adapting. We are learning how to exist and survive utilizing unconventional measures that have become our "new normal."

Good Disruption and Bad Disruption

When it comes to disruption, there is good disruption and bad disruption. Good disruption is the process of making that which was normal better; it suggests change for the better in processes, thought, and practices. On the other hand, bad disruption means that necessary things are disrupted and produces chaos and scrambling for normalcy and consistency. This season of global disruption due to the COVID-19 pandemic caused entire countries to shut down for months, which had a devastating effect on the health community and global economics.

COVID-19 was both a good and bad disruptor. Because of the shutdown, many businesses did not survive. They had to either file bankruptcy or just throw in the towel and put up the white flag of surrender. Companies have amassed massive debt due to accruing physical expenses while moving their operations to cyberspace and virtual interaction through technology, which had its new costs. The way that businesses have operated in the past, by necessity or disruption, has changed and impacted the economy. Because of this disruption, unemployment rates have soared to rates unseen since the Great Depression. To add insult to our economic injury, we have entered into a constitutional disruption. Americans demand justice based upon the rise and continued murder of people of color by the hands of law enforcement that has culminated in protest. So, while in America alone with over nine million cases of coronavirus and over 600,000 deaths, our country is in political turmoil.

As a good disruptor, many have prospered from the pandemic, and others will continue to prosper. The pandemic has been a boom for technology retailers, delivery services, etc.; however, most of your small companies and medium companies will continue to struggle and close their doors. Unfortunately, the church was not exempt. In the church community,

those ahead of the technology curve thrived; others could not adapt and closed. For some churches, members stopped contributing to the church either through loss of income or loss of interest.

While the 2020 disruption that has manifested effects upon 2021 has been devastating, there is an upside to disruption. Disruption presents entrepreneurial opportunities for new companies to enter the market and present innovation, creativity, and transition products for which the new reality has created a demand. Larger companies tend to be too large to make quick adjustments in their equipment and processes to change to meet current demands and supply needs. So let's delve a little deeper from our discussion about natural disruption to spiritual disruption.

The church has been impacted possibly more than any other large-scale company. It was considered non-essential at the beginning of the pandemic, and people were directly instructed not to attend church because of social distancing. Many church services have been moved to online only for over 15 months and counting. This distance has created an enormous challenge for the Christian church because the nature of the church is physical. Virtual worship can complement physical worship but not replace it. During this Kingdom disruption or the disruption of the church, statistics suggest that by the end of 2021, one-third of the church will not return and will close their doors.

Kingdom Disruption and Falling Away

I believe that this disruption is a Kingdom disruption – the great falling away that the Apostle Paul discussed in 1 Timothy 4:1. I believe we are witnessing the signs of the time that Jesus discussed in His Olivet Discourse in Matthew 24 and the signs discussed in the Petrine and Pauline epistles. I believe that we are living in the days of eschatology and that the blowing of the trumpet for the church (1 Thessalonians 4:16) is imminent. With this being said, I believe that revival and reformation will take place right before this time. God will send a revival that complements the knock on the door of the church in Revelation 3:20.

I believe that a tremendous harvest for the Kingdom is lying dormant for a relationship with Christ and the church. This Kingdom disruption will be a revival that begins in the church. Jesus is calling people who have been blinded and deceived by Satan, who poses as an angel of light. I believe that this disruption allowed people, who relied on physical activity to define their walk with God, to now focus on what they believe. COVID-19, with the threat of death and under isolation, caused people to go to social media to hear the Word of God since it was the primary means to hear preaching. Online church caused adaptive and capable preachers to cut the fluff and entertainment and focus on the pure unadulterated Word of God. The hungry saints ate and

are eating, but there are more, the elect, in need of revival and the ingathering!

During this disruption, I believe that the church has
been given an opportunity to take advantage of the
following during this Kingdom disruption:

Kingdom Disruption Opportunities	
1.	The usage and the literacy of technology
2.	The ability to reach people we could never reach physically in our churches through social media
3.	To become more efficient in our administration by utilizing technology to meet with our people
4.	To engage in online discipleship that can increase people's opportunity to participate in discipleship
5.	To create a hybrid community and expand the church's reach and vision
6.	To engage in the Great Commission and connect with ministries in other countries
7.	To engage in end-time ministries through technology

While I could list several opportunities that the church
can take advantage of during this Kingdom disruption,
these seven are the starting point. This is a tremen-

dous opportunity for the church to take advantage of change and become more innovative and creative concerning Kingdom disruption!

Online Church: To Be or Not to Be

Today, we are being called to lead in what I refer to as a "disrupted church culture." You and I have been called to be leaders of the 21st century disrupted church culture and a disrupted world. So I believe that one of the greatest questions facing the church today is can a person be a part of a church through online technology since the church is only the church in physical gathering.

I know many people are convinced that a temporary solution can become the final solution for church participation. If it worked for a year plus, why can't it work for a lifetime? An examination of Israel and their exilic experience reveals to us that they could not continue to exist away from their gathering place. It was only when they got back to Jerusalem, their homeland, and the place of the Temple that they could thrive as God's people and be who they were created to be in the world. So can you be a part of a church through online participation since you did it through COVID-19? The answer is yes and no.

First, let me begin addressing this question in layers. The first layers are those who are local members of the church. If you are a local partner of the church, you are mandated to physical gatherings unless you have a valid reason for not attending (work, sickness, vacation, etc.). But as soon as this period ends, you are expected to be in assembly. Remember, as I discussed through-out the book, there are many reasons why we gather beyond accountability. It's not simply about finances; to be honest, for many churches, including mine, the finances stayed at the same level or increased during the pandemic. You need physical gathering if you will continue to be who you are called to be in the unity of the community and the relationship of fellowship. The physical gathering is more than simply coming to church on Sunday morning; it is committing and submitting to your local church based upon Kingdom protocols. And it is embracing the gifts of covering and community for your personal and community sustain-ability. If you cannot make worship services or other activities, then online ministry services should be tak-en advantage of because of your inability to be physi-cally present.

Distant Online Members
The next level is those who have been reached through streaming services and have connected with a cover-ing or church leader and become an online member. Now the question is, how can one truly be an online member without physical gathering in that the church is the church in gathering? Can I be a valid online church member? Yes and no! Yes, if you are going to be genuinely connected to your church to the point that

you've created cyber-kinesthetic moments of touch. What this means is, if you are going to be a valid online church member that is a part of the local church and online community, which is one and the same, you must be totally immersed in the community life of the church. There is no such thing as authentic church membership without participation in the whole. This is the distinction between the visible and the invisible church, those who participate and those who don't. If you are indeed a part of the invisible church, you will be active in the visible church.

Seven in 10 church adults (70%) agree that digital resources should be used to reach and engage their neighborhoods. There is an incredible opportunity to participate in the Great Commission online. Getting involved in the community of the local church requires becoming fully vested in the unity of community. You must desire to know and be known by the community, not simply a surreptitious or secret member.

The following is a list of suggestions that can assist with integrating online members into the community of the local church so that there may be the unity of community as online members:

1. **You must formally join the local church as an online member and participate in the church's new member processes.** The church must have its new member processes offered online to integrate online members into full membership of the church through the unity of community.

2. **You must become financially accountable by engaging in stewardship through tithes, offerings, etc.** The ministry must have a technological process that allows people to give online and stay accountable for their contributions.

3. **You must engage in small group ministries, if available.** This is where discipleship takes place, as well as relationship-making and building.

4. **You must participate in online Sunday worship services weekly.** This is low-hanging fruit, but the church must offer interactive worship experiences. This is where an online pastor must be integrated into the live stream to communicate with online members.

5. **You must attend weekly online Bible study with your leader.** If you are serious about wanting to be a part of the assembly or engaged in the unity of community, you need to attend online Bible study. The more your presence is known online, people in the community will become more familiar with you. It will show when you get involved in other areas of ministry, like small groups.

6. **Connect with an online coordinator for online members to develop accountability and connection.** If you want to be a part of the community, you must reach out and communicate every opportunity you can. You don't just want to

know your church online; you want your church to know you. The online member must be more intentional and aggressive about connecting to the local church community.

7. **Attend church conferences, events, and activities at least two to three times a year to establish physical relationships with the church leaders who watch for your soul.** There must be moments of touch if you intend to genuinely be a part of the physical community of faith. You must travel to your church for baptism and other special events to actually touch your shepherd and the members with whom you share time in online discipleship groups and online ministry involvement.

There must be some physical exchange – even Paul, who was not a local church pastor, desired physical touches with the churches that he planted. So these are some suggestions that I highly recommend for churches to employ to close the digital divide if you want to truly establish unity through community.

Unfortunately, most of the arguments being made for online church have been offered by those who are not willing to participate in the community life of the church. However, Paul clearly lays out God's expectation for the local church under His delegated leaders: the purpose, mandates, and benefits of the church community in Ephesians 4:11-16:

> *"Furthermore, He gave some people as emissaries, some as prophets, some as proclaimers of the Good News, and some as shepherds and teachers. Their task is to equip God's people for the work of service that builds the body of the Messiah, until we all arrive at the*

unity implied by trusting and knowing the Son of God, at full manhood, at the standard of maturity set by the Messiah's perfection. We will then no longer be infants tossed about by the waves and blown along by every wind of teaching, at the mercy of people clever in devising ways to deceive. Instead, speaking the truth in love, we will in every respect grow up into him who is the head, the Messiah. Under his control, the whole body is being fitted and held together by the support of every joint, with each part working to fulfill its function; this is how the body grows and builds itself up in love."

The Hybrid Church Model

The Hybrid Church Model is a church model that can be used to supplement physical gathering. It is a way to incorporate online members into an existing physical community through the unity of community. The Hybrid Church is not a convenience church; it is a church that utilizes technology to engage distant members in the unity of community. The Hybrid Church Model provides a way for the church membership to execute in the Great Commission worldwide, ensuring the interconnectedness of the church online and on-campus. The Hybrid Church Model provides online members with the necessary discipleship they need to embrace the work of ministry.

During our discussion of the importance of physical gathering, we concluded from biblical teachings that the church must operate in the unity of community. So the goal of the Hybrid Church Model, which is the inclusion and merging of the online community with the on-campus community, is to establish one unified church that is comprised of both online and on-campus members. All that the on-campus ministry is, the online ministry is. Every ministry opportunity that is available to the on-campus people is offered the same or similarly online. All of the goods and services of the ministry are provided to the entire membership, online and on-campus. Through the utilization of cutting-edge technology, ministry opportunities and gatherings will be made available to the entire congregation, which will serve as the substratum of the Hybrid Church Model.

When we speak of hybrid, we're speaking of the design of a thing, made by combining two different elements – a mixture of the two components. I strongly recommend the Hybrid Church Model for ministries that desire not to have two separate churches – one online and the other on-campus. I believe that it is more consistent with the biblical model of the unity of community when we employ a hybrid model that involves bringing the two spheres together in community through technology. To not lose the momentum and the interest of those who are not a part of our local geography,

the Hybrid Church Model of 21st century ministry, post-COVID, blends the in-person culture with the online culture.

The Hybrid Church Model is not simply streaming services; it is the actual offer of church in the unity of community in a physical AND digital environment, which I call the "phygital" experience. Barna Research Group states, "One in five churched adults has what

Barna calls "high digital openness." Looking ahead, millennial churchgoers say hybrid church, just as much as physical church, will be a good fit for them. However, it is important to mention their research also states, "81 percent of churched adults say it's very important to them to worship God in person and alongside others. More than half of churched adults say that post-pandemic, primarily physical services will best suit their life."

Barna's research solidifies that online church must extend beyond streaming Sunday services online. His research states that 60% of those participating in a church that offers online services during the pandemic say this is the only digital offering the church makes available.[4] Sixty-three percent of churched adults believe churches should use digital resources for purposes of spiritual formation and discipleship. When we develop a robust hybrid experience, it creates a holistic experience for the entire community — not simply watchman-ship but membership that functions in the unity of community. The church must not ignore the harvest of people who have not walked into the doors of the church. Yet, we must be open to the harvest God brought from COVID digitally, who were and are willing to listen in the comfort of their own homes. Their digital interest can become the starting point for their spiritual journey to the unity of community. The church has to be strategic in its approach of attracting and engaging online viewers through online evangelism.

It's important to understand how many people now are open to online church. In fact, 67% of churches that never streamed before COVID-19 now offer services online. People are more open to online services than

4 Barna.com. *What Churches Might Miss When Measuring Digital Attendance*, Retrieved from https://www.barna.com/research/watching-online-church/

ever before. However, 81% of churched adults say that it's imperative to them to experience God alongside others at a physical church gathering. It is clear that if we don't offer the Hybrid Church Model of 21st century ministry, we will miss a tremendous opportunity to engage a new generation of church members.

To offer a healthy hybrid model, there must be the appointment or assignment of an online pastor or coordinator responsible for connecting with online members and leading them down the path of community. The Hybrid Church Model ensures that membership extends beyond Sunday and provides a church without walls experience. The Hybrid Church Model ensures that online members have multiple levels of connection to the entire membership to create the unity of community. There must be intentional efforts to connect with the online community through streaming and in an online fellowship room after the services for those who would like to share with the online pastor and online team.

There is no such thing as authentic church membership without participation in the whole. Once again, this is the distinction between the visible and the invisible church; those who participate and those who don't. If you are indeed a part of the invisible church, you will be active in the visible church. It is my strong theological and biblical conclusion that we gather for the following reasons:

Because...

1. That is who we are; our identity is in our gathering; we are the assembly.
2. As a physical gathering of people, we represent

the Kingdom of God upon the earth as a king-dom of priests (Exodus 19:6). We are God's peo-ple for possession.

3. We are a spiritual nation, not persons; we are a holy nation. We are in the world, but our place is not of the world; we belong with each other.

4. God has called us to both a vertical relationship with Him and a horizontal relationship with each other. We were created to love both God and neighbor in the unity of community.

5. Just as Israel represented the Kingdom of God among men, so does the gathered church.

6. The Newer Testament church is a gathering church, and everyone who was being saved was added to the physical gathering.

7. We are a part of the invisible church of the elect who gather in the world to represent God to the world.

8. There is power in the unity of community.

9. We are safe and have a sense of protection in the community with our covering, even from false prophets and prophecies.

10. Fellowship is a priority in the Kingdom.

11. Things happen supernaturally when we are gathered that don't take place in other atmo-spheres,

12. We must have a context in which we are trained, discipled, and assigned ministry opportunities.

This is a prophetic season marked by the preaching of the gospel of the Kingdom around the world as a witness, and then shall the end come (Matthew 24:14). We must reach people globally and possess the abil-ity to disciple laymen, church leaders, and churches through technology. While we cannot be there, we can use technology to continue to reach those who are not in our geographical reach.

Conclusion

It is my prayer that every believer discovers the joy and significance of being a part of the Body of Christ and corporate gathering. We must love the brethren and strengthen and encourage one another to press towards the higher gathering in the eternal Kingdom of God. In essence, go to church, love the saints, be connected to the community, and keep the faith. This is the season of endurance; Jesus said those who would endure to the end are those that will inherit eternal life. It is your church community that will assist you in making it to the end without compromise. Now, these three remain – faith, hope, and love, but the greatest is love (1 Corinthians 13:13)!

> *...not neglecting our own congregational meetings, as some have made a practice of doing, but, rather, encouraging each other. And let us do this all the more as you see the Day approaching. – Hebrews 10:25-26*

ABOUT DR. DANA CARSON

As a Pastor

Dr. Dana Carson is the Senior Pastor of the Reflections of Christ's Kingdom World Outreach International — a Bible-centered, Spirit-filled, Community-building, Kingdom-minded mega-ministry in Houston, TX. Dr. Carson is one of the nation's foremost Kingdom theologians and down-to-earth pastors whose radical message and raw delivery are known all over the world. R.O.C.K. Sunday morning worship services are unlike anything seen in the Body of Christ – exciting, cutting-edge, extraordinary, and anointed – utilizing all of the tools and technology of our current age to present the timeless message of the gospel of the Kingdom of God!

The R.O.C.K has a profound focus on the spiritual and educational empowerment of children and youth, which birthed from Dr. Carson overcoming the odds of Chicago inner city life as an African American boy. His life inspires the next generation to become Kingdom leaders in government, education, business, church, and family. Dr. Carson's anointing represents a combination of Spirit-filled fire and formal academic training, with a touch of the lessons learned in the ghettos of Chicago. Combining biblical study and scholarship, Dr. Carson is frank and real – people love the way he teaches the practical application of the Word of God on a level that anyone and everyone can understand. Dr. Carson is a Kingdom-driven man on a Kingdom mission, possessing an apostolic calling, profound pastoral insight, and nearly 40 years of ministry experience.

As an Apostle With a Prophetic Voice

God set Dr. Carson aside to be a significant leader in the Kingdom Reformation Movement. He is world-renowned for his expertise on the Kingdom of God (the Kingdom Voice), emphasizing its Jewish context, and its message of the power of the Holy Spirit, apostolic order, sonship, and service. Holding firmly to the mandate in Matthew 28 that commissions all believers to go and teach all nations, Dr. Carson has identified, equipped, planted, and oversees hundreds of Bible-centered, Spirit-filled, Community-building, Kingdom-minded leaders and churches on four continents – North America, Africa, Europe, and Asia, with the vision of planting R.O.C.K. churches on every inhabitable continent in over 120 countries! An apostle, defined by the Bible, he has established three church campuses in the Houston and Greater Houston area - Broadway, Edgebrook, Alvin, as well as lead the church to purchase and payoff 221 acres just 30 minutes south of downtown Houston. Dr. Carson has also trained leaders in doctrine and planted several R.O.C.K. churches in Virginia, Georgia, Illinois, and Texas, as well as over 100 churches in South Africa, Poland, Liberia, and India. In recognition of his exemplary works in ministry, the 2007 Theologian Awards Production and the Tour of Hope Foundation awarded Dr. Carson with the Five-Fold Ministry Award. In 2023, Dr. Carson received the "Scholar-Practitioner" award, as one of the top 50 influencers of Pentecostalism in the world, from the Black Alliance of Pentecostal Scholars and Oral Roberts University.

As a Scholar

Dr. Carson, though a high school dropout from Chicago, has earned three doctorates and four master degrees, thus he is one of the top 1% of African American scholars in the U.S. Dr. Carson earned a Doctorate of Ministry from Boston University and also studied The Church and Economic and Community Development at the Harvard Graduate School of Divinity. He also earned a Doctorate of Christian Psychology from Logos Graduate School. In 2004, Dr. Carson completed a Ph.D. in Organizational Leadership from Regent University. He also holds four master's degrees: a Master in Counseling and Guidance (Texas A&M), a Master of Divinity (Austin Presbyterian Theological Seminary/Oral Roberts University), Master of Economic Development and Entrepreneurship (University of Houston), and he was the first full-time clergy to earn a Global Executive MBA from the world-class Fuqua School of Business (Duke University). Dr. Carson received his B.S. in Business Administration from HBCU Wiley United Methodist College where he became a member of Kappa Alpha Psi Fraternity, Inc.

Author, Entrepreneur, and Leadership Expert

Dr. Carson is the Chief Executive Visionary and founder of Dana Carson Kingdom Ministries, Inc. (DCKM), a non-profit ministry organization designed to spread the gospel of the Kingdom while restoring families and communities through programs of empowerment. Through DCKM, Dr. Carson spreads the good news of the Kingdom around the world through preaching, education, and literature. Dr. Dana Carson is a prolific author and writer of biblical study guides and curricula. He has written numerous books in theology, leadership, and church growth. Dr. Carson has authored over 200 books/Kingdom resources that are designed to help transform believers in every aspect of their walk with God. However, DCKM is only one of several companies that have been established to resource and support the expansion of God's Kingdom. Many of his books are used to train leaders and laypeople in the Kingdom Bible University (KBU) and the Kingdom Theological Seminary, of which he is the founder and chancellor. This 21st century transformational leader's organizational expertise impacts business professionals in addition to church leadership. An entrepreneur in his own right, he owns several additional businesses: Carson Consulting Group; IntelliChurchTM Ministry Solutions; and FD's Famous Burgers and Chicago-Style Wings.

Dr. Carson conducts professional leadership seminars to community, church, and business leaders worldwide. He is the chief leadership strategist at the DCKM Leadership Development & Training Corporation, a training company that equips and empowers leaders through state-of-the-art leadership coaching seminars. Also a certified church growth specialist, Dr. Carson advises pastors and ministries how to holistically increase their membership according to God's design — reviving, revitalizing, and redirecting churches toward healthy growth for effective ministry. Dr. Carson also provides leadership training through the Center for Church Growth and Kingdom Empowerment, which assists churches across denominational lines, cultural lines, and generational lines, but is especially dedicated to a very unique market of churches and church leaders – African Americans.

Community-Builder

Dr. Carson's fervor for lifting, developing, and building communities is second to none. Dr. Carson studied the church, economics, and community building during his doctoral studies at Harvard University. Dr. Carson wrote his dissertation on the relationship between African American males between the ages of 14-35 and the independent church at Boston University, the alma mater of the distinguished Martin Luther King Jr. and C. Eric Lincoln. Wherever the Lord plants him, Dr. Carson establishes a vibrant ministry that touches the lives of people – mind, body, and soul. In Houston, the vision of The R.O.C.K. and the ministry of Dr. Dana Carson has always been characterized by community activism, community development, and economic empowerment through life skills training. The R.O.C.K. has provided toys, backpacks, school supplies, face masks, transportation, skills development, food, and hurricane relief to the citizens of the southeast Houston area. Dr. Carson provides mentorship and exposure opportunities through at-risk programs for junior high and high school youth, and a special mentor programs for young males of color including the Carson Male Academy and the Young Prophets and Ministers. For his many efforts, President Barack Obama selected him to receive the President's Lifetime Achievement Award, the most prestigious given to a few Americans in recognition of over 4,000 hours of extraordinary service! In 2016, God gave Dr. Carson perhaps his most significant assignment – the opportunity to acquire a Christian elementary school in Nairobi, Kenya that educates almost 500 disadvantaged and unserved children in the Mukuru Kwa Njenga slum.

Evangelist and Revivalist
Internationally renowned, Dr. Carson ministers extensively through seminars, crusades, social media, and television where his preaching and teaching has been broadcast on TBN, BET, Daystar, the WORD Network, satellite television (the Omega Channel and IMPACT Network) in over 62 countries in Africa and Europe; and primetime TV. His broadcasts on radio (Rainbow

FM 90.7 (Johannesburg, SA), Sunny 88.7 FM (Accra, GH), and KWWJ Gospel 1360 AM (Houston, TX); and TV (Chicago, Detroit, Ghana, and Houston Media Source – Comcast, AT&T U-verse, TVMax, Sudden Link, and Phonoscope) have and are providing invaluable knowledge and understanding for pastors and laymen worldwide. Dr. Carson has been a guest on the Yolanda Adams Morning Show; the Houston Newsmakers, hosted by Khambrel Marshall; and Sunday Morning Live on the Majic 102.1 Show. He is the innovator for the highly successful Relevant Pulpits and Kingdom Voice Live shows on the YouTube Channel – Apostle Dr. Dana Carson, Facebook, and www.TheROCKWOI.com

As a Father and Husband

Dr. Carson is a devoted husband to Lady Rachelle Carson, who serves faithfully in ministry with him as Executive Pastor of The R.O.C.K. World Outreach in Houston, Dean of the Kingdom Theological Seminary, and Chief Editor of Dana Carson Kingdom Ministries. He affectionately calls her "Baruch." They have been blessed with five children: Dana Carson II, John Anthony Carson, Angel Naomi Carson, Marielle Alli Sanchez, and Devon Jarrod Carson.

ADDITIONAL KINGDOM BOOKS

If you are a person who is serious about walking with the King and fulfilling the King's preordained purpose you were birthed for, Dr. Dana Carson has penned the following works as a labor of love to assist you in your transformation. In order to fully understand the Kingdom to the point where you can explain it and teach it to others, these books are "must reads."

The Five Watersheds of History & Theology

ISBN: 978-1-940264-86-8

The Five (5) Watersheds of History and Theology takes a fresh look into 21st Century Christianity in light of cultural distortions and the Kingdom of God. The Bible is the bestselling book of all times and is used as the source document of Christianity. The Bible has touched cultures all over the world and has been the substratum for both the Roman Catholic church and the Protestant Church. The challenge facing the 21st century church attrition rate and the decline of interest in attending church, particularly in Europe, Australia, and North America has led to many becoming atheist or pursuing other religious perspectives. Why are so many revisiting their commitment to the Christian faith? Many people today approach Christianity, and now the Bible, with great skepticism due to the great racial and cultural divide that is associated with Christianity. The Five Watersheds of History and Theology explores how the, once polarizing, Christian faith has lost its impact over time in spite of having such powerful historical roots. This book examines how the central theme of the Bible, "The Kingdom of God," in its Jewish context, which was the original context in which God chose to communicate His message, lost its cultural influences and context. There are five watersheds (an event or period marking a turning point in a course of action or state of affairs), that have totally reshaped the message of the Bible and the scriptures, and has distorted the biblical view of God, Romanization, Europeanization, Colonization, Westernization, and Americanization of the Gospel. These Five Watersheds have made tremendous impacts upon the Christian faith-- some positive and some negative. You will learn how the faith was formulated and distorted through socio-economics, politics and race; and what necessary amendments are needed to our current approach to the faith.

Welcome to the Kingdom

ISBN: 978-1-940264-57-8

What does it really mean to be in the Kingdom? Today, one of the biggest hindrances to entering the Kingdom is joining the church. While the church is a critical organism in the Kingdom, it was never intended to be the ultimate in the Kingdom. In this Kingdom work, Welcome to the Kingdom, Dr. Carson clearly and practically teaches on what it means to see, enter, and live a Kingdom life!

Using the Kingdom Parable of the Sower, Dr. Carson teaches you how to be a victorious Kingdom citizen over Satan and situations. You will learn:

- The difference between the church and the Kingdom
- The Kingdom message and mission in a 21st century context
- How the enemy strategically attacks your life
- The four key Kingdom relationships of EVERY Kingdom citizen

Welcome to the Kingdom will help you as a 21st century believer understand your Kingdom citizenship, making it one of the most practical books written on the Kingdom of God ever!

Whether you're a leader or a laymen, this book will revolutionize your life! Welcome to the Kingdom and welcome to the abundant and prosperous Kingdom life!

The Kingdom, Then, Now, and to Come!

ISBN: 978-1-9402645-9-2

The Kingdom Then, Now, and to Come is one of Dr. Dana Carson's most brilliant works on the Kingdom of God.

In this scholarly work, Dr. Carson explores and examines the historical positions on the Kingdom of God and reveals how the Kingdom is not relegated to the past (then) nor restricted to the future (to come), but is available in the right NOW!

Through the power of the Holy Spirit, you, as the enforcer of the Kingdom, can heal the sick, cast out devils, raise the dead, and empower the poor NOW!

We we guarantee that you will not be able to put this work down once you open the latest and perhaps the most persuasive and compelling book written by Dr. Dana Carson, the Kingdom Voice, and one of the foremost Kingdom scholars in the 21st century!

And This Gospel of the Kingdom: Re-interpreting the Gospel in a Post-Colonial Context

ISBN: 0-9746616-3-5

And This Gospel of the Kingdom is another brilliant work from the pen and spirit of Dr. Carson. In this book, he revisits the traditional view of the gospel of the Kingdom of God and concludes that we have proclaimed the gospel with a misaligned emphasis placed upon the death, burial, and resurrection of Christ.

He thoroughly proves, from the Holy Scriptures through the dispensations of time, that Christ came preaching the gospel of the Kingdom, not the gospel of the resurrection.

Dr. Carson opines that the message of the cross and the resurrection was never intended to be the end goal, but the means to the end – the Kingdom! This book:

Explains how the gospel has been misinterpreted and that the authentic gospel of the Kingdom calls men to subject themselves to the rule and reign of God through Christ Jesus.

Reveals that God desires and it is His will to become Lord, not just Savior, of the believer's life – the new dominating force in life that fills the void left by Satan's dominion.

This is a must read for every serious believer and church leader! It will surely cause you to re-evaluate your belief in the work of Christ as the Passover Lamb and re-evaluate your commitment to Jesus the Messiah!

The Crown and the Cross: Understanding the Kingdom of God

ISBN: 978-1-9402643-8-7

The Crown and the Cross: Understanding the Kingdom of God will be one of the best books you will ever read concerning understanding the Kingdom of God! Undoubtedly, The Crown and the Cross will revolutionize the way you define your faith. Dr. Dana Carson is considered the world's foremost Kingdom scholar, who has written over one hundred books and study guides that help the believer live the Kingdom life. After reading

The Crown and the Cross, your practical walk with God will never be the same as Dr. Carson challenges you to rethink your interpretation of scripture based upon a Kingdom perspective that highlights the crown of Christ and not merely the cross of Christ! This book will open the minds of those who have been trapped in traditional views of the church that cause stagnation and disinterest. We invite you to explore a fresh look at the cross of Christ through the lens of the crown of Christ and become empowered to live a victorious life in the Kingdom! This is an investment you will never be sorry you made! YOU MUST READ THIS BOOK!

Kingdom Reformation

ISBN: 978-1-940264-63-9

This book walks you through the history of the Christian faith in the Old and New Testament through the history of the modern church until today. The Kingdom Reformation also observes the current condition and the future of the church from both a scriptural and prophetic perspective of change and reformation. This book is a must-read for saints who want to understand the prophetic clock of God regarding the church and eschatology. Have we entered into the final dispensation of theological renewal?

This book will assist you in both your witness and discipleship in the world and in the church! We know that this work will bless pastors, church leaders, small groups, academic classrooms, serious readers, and truth seekers! Thank you, Dr. Dana Carson, the Kingdom Voice, for your reformational and revolutionary teachings on the Kingdom of God.

Dr. Carson has authored over 200 books and Bible studies guides. Visit shop.DrDanaCarson.com for more resources.